The Picture Rulebook of KIDS' GAMES

The Picture Rulebook of KIDS' GAMES

Roxanne Henderson

Illustrated by Michael Brown

Produced by the Philip Lief Group, Inc.

CONTEMPORARY BOOKS
A TRIBUNE NEW MEDIA/EDUCATION COMPANY

Library of Congress Cataloging-in-Publication Data

Henderson, Roxanne.
  The picture rulebook of kids' games : over 200 favorites, from
alphabet objects to zookeeper, fully illustrated and organized
for easy reference / Roxanne Henderson.
      p.   cm.
  ISBN 0-8092-3227-8
  1. Games—Rules.   2. Games—Rules—Pictorial works.
  I. Title.
  GV1201.42.B76   1996   95-48389
  790.1'922—dc20   CIP

Front cover design by Monica Baziuk
Interior design by Hespenheide Design

Published by Contemporary Books, Inc.
Two Prudential Plaza, Chicago, Illinois 60601-6790
Manufactured in the United States of America
International Standard Book Number: 0-8092-3227-8
10   9   8   7   6   5   4   3   2   1

This book is dedicated to our son, Graham,

who got us back to playing games

and who understood wonderfully most of those times

when we were too busy writing and drawing games

to play them with him.

Contents

Introduction, 1

Adverbally, 3

Alphabet Objects, 4

Anagrams, 5

Apple Bobbing, 6

Arm Wrestling, 7

Assassin, 8

Backlash, 9

Bad Sport's Race, 10

Ball and Caps, 11

Ball Duck Race, 12

Ball Tag, 13

Ball Volley, 14

Balloon Duo, 15

Battle at Sea, 16

Beanbag Toss, 18

Bicycle Beanbag Balance, 19

Bicycle Coast Race, 20

Bicycle Slalom Race, 21

Bicycle Un-Race, 22

Bingo, 23

Bingo for Preschoolers, 24

Black Magic, 25

Blindman's Buff, 26

Botticelli, 27

Brooklyn Bridge, 28

Bubble Blow Race, 29

Cardywinks, 30

Cat and Mouse, 31

Catch a Cootie, 32

Categories, 34

Caterpillar, 35

Chain Story, 37

Charades, 38

Chicken Fights, 42

Cootie-Bug, 43

Cracker Race, 44

Crazy Eights, 45

Cross Tag, 47

Deadly Queen, 48

Dodge War, 49

Dodgeball, 50

Dodgeball Reverse, 51

Drop Dead, 52

Drop the Hankie, 53

Duck, Duck, Goose, 54

Egg or Water-Balloon Toss, 55

Egg Polo, 56

Exquisite Corpse, 57

Farmer, Farmer, May We Cross?, 58

Follow-Up Goal, 60

Four Square, 62

Fox and Hen, 63

Freeze Tag, 64

Frisbee Golf, 65

Fruit Basket, 66

German, 67

German Singles, 69

Goal Kickers, 70

Grab Tag, 72

Greedy, 73

Greek Ball, 74

Hand Tennis, 75

Hand Wrestling, 76

Handball, 77

Hangman, 79

Hat Thieves, 81

Hide-and-Seek, 82

Hide-and-Seek and Go Home, 83

Hide the Button, 84

Homonyms, 85

Homonym Detective, 86

Homonyms in the Teakettle, 87

Hopscotch, 88

Horse, 91

Hot Potato, 92

Huckleberry Finn, 93

Hundred-Mile Race, 94

I Doubt It, 95

I Spy, 96

Indian Ball, 97

Jacks, 98

Jambalaya Relay, 104

Jingle Tag, 105

Keep-Away, 106

Kick the Can, 107

Killer Whale, 109

King of the Hill, 110

Lean-Two, 112

Leapfrog, 113

London Bridge, 115

Marbles, 117

Marco Polo, 128

Memory, 130

Milk Caps, 131

Minicroquet, 137

Mnemonics, 138

Moby Dick, 139

Monkey in the Middle, 140

Mother, May I?, 141

Mousetrap, 143

Mulberry Bush, 144

Musical Chairs, 146

Obstacle Course, 148

Octopus, 149

Paper Airplane Race, 150

Pass Ball, 151

Peanut Race, 152

Pie Tag, 153

Pig in the Pen, 155

Poison, 156

Poison Ball, 158

Potato Relay, 160

Prisoner Base, 161

Punch Ball, 163

Rabbit, 164

Rattlesnake, 165

Red Light, Green Light, 166

Red Rover, 167

Relay Race (Classic Version), 168

Ring-Around-the-Rosy, 170

Rosemary, 171

'Round the World, 172

Run for Your Supper, 173

Safe Tag, 174

Safety Zones, 175

Sardines, 176

Scavenger Hunt, 178

Scissors, Paper, Stone, 180

Seven Up, 181

Shadow Tag, 183

Shark and Minnows, 184

Sheep, Sheep, Come Home, 185

Shopping Trip, 186

Sidewalk Golf, 187

Simon Says, 188

Simon Says *Not*, 189

Skate Obstacle Course, 190

Soccer Tag, 191

Spell It How? (Llep Stiw Oh?), 192

Spoons, 193

Spud, 194

Squareball, 196

Statues, 198

Tag, 199

Teacher's Cat, 200

Telephone Message, 201

Tell a Tale, 202

Three Words, 203

Throw and Go, 204

Thumb Wrestling, 205

Tic-Tac-Toe, 206

Tic-Tac-Toe Four, 207

Toss Ball, 208

Tree Ball, 209

Trips, 211

Trips, Jr., 213

Tug-of-War, 215

Twenty Questions, 216

Twenty-One, 217

Ultimate Frisbee, 219

Underwater Tag, 221

Virginia Woolf, 222

Volcano, 223

Volleyballoon, 224

Wall of China, 225

War, 226

War Times Two, 227

Water Brigade, 228

Water Hoops, 229

Water Volleyball, 230

Watermelon Ball, 232

What's Missing?, 233

What's the Time, Mr. Wolf?, 234

Wheeled Toss-in Race, 235

Word Association, 236

Word War, 237

Zookeeper, 238

The Picture Rulebook of KIDS' GAMES

Introduction

From the moment when an infant first recognizes "Peek-a-boo, I see you!" children understand that games are fun. As kids grow up, their games become more sophisticated, and their circle of playmates expands beyond their parents and siblings to their friends and schoolmates. Nothing later in life compares to the hours children spend playing games!

If we're lucky, we never outgrow the love of game playing. When our own children come along, we revisit childhood for a while, remembering and enjoying again those youthful pastimes. Sometimes, though, recalling the rules to all of these games can be difficult. This book is designed to help you out, and at the same time it will provide you with clever new entertainments.

Rules are important. Players must know what a game is about before they can play it, and the rules provide the boundaries and set the guidelines so everyone understands what is expected of them. The very fun of games is built into their rules, and rules help keep the fun fair and safe.

Of course, there is no one perfect or perfectly right way to play many of the games in this book. Indeed, rules shouldn't be a straitjacket, stifling the enjoyment of the activity. Once players learn the basics, they can be open-minded. If the people in a group think they would enjoy bending the rules, ignoring some, or writing some new ones, and everyone agrees, great!

What's in This Book

This book outlines the rules of more than two hundred kids' games and variations. It will refresh your memory, teach you a new thing or two, and become the indispensable source of countless hours of joy for the children in your life.

We have steered away from games that have many and complex rules. Many books have already been published on the details of sports like basketball, baseball, and soccer. When we do include a game that has a complicated, official version (such as Handball), we offer a streamlined version for a friendly game.

The activities featured in *The Picture Rulebook of Kids' Games* range from Blindman's Buff to Charades, from Crazy Eights to Horse, from Marco Polo to Mother, May I? We have also included some pastimes you may have never encountered: Three Words, for instance.

There are games of cards, jacks, and marbles; games to play in the living room, gym, car, backyard, and pool; and quickie games to play on the baseball diamond or basketball court with just a friend or two. There's plenty, too, for the preschool players in the family.

In this book, you'll learn how to create homemade versions of popular games like Battleship and Cootie, a few unique ways to spend a rainy day, and some classic rough-and-tumble activities that can be played by an entire fourth grade. Some of the games are ancient. Prisoner Base dates back to England in the 1300s, Blindman's Buff to ancient Greece. But we also include a section on the evolving rules for the latest craze, Milk Caps (a.k.a. POGS). Best of all, most games in *The Picture Rulebook of Kids' Games* require no special, expensive equipment or exotic supplies, just a ball or a Frisbee, or a pen and paper.

There's something for everyone!

How to Use This Book

This book is organized in an accessible, alphabetized format, from Adverbally to Zookeeper. This makes it easy for you to look up a particular game. For Hide-and-Seek, look under *H*; if you want to read about Ring-Around-the-Rosy, go to *R*. Some game sections (Marbles, Jacks, and others) include a number of variations alphabetized within them. For those interested in a listing of games by category—for example, Ball Games for Big Groups or Mind, Word, and Memory Games—see the Subject Index at the end of the book.

The beginning of each entry lists pertinent facts about each game. First, we specify the type of game it is—ball, swimming pool, party guessing game, etc. Next, you will learn what the object of the game is, how many players are needed, and what age range of players is recommended. (Sometimes, instead of age, we give a skill requirement. After all, to take part in bicycle contests, age doesn't matter if the player can't ride a bike!) Entries also indicate where to play the games—indoors, outdoors, in a car, in a pool—and what equipment is needed.

Who Goes First?

Many of the games start out with instructions to choose a player to be It, or to decide who'll go first. How do players do this? In our family, we let the youngest go first. But there are lots of other tried-and-true methods. Here are some suggestions:

- Throw dice. The high or low number goes first.
- Choose a card. The high or low card goes first.
- Pull straws. The short or long one goes first.
- Play Scissors, Paper, Stone.
- Toss a coin. Heads or tails goes first.

Or just take turns going first!

Have Fun!

Everyone loves to win, but learning to be a good sport is important, too. Above all, when playing a game, parents, grandparents, kids, teachers, and friends should emphasize simple enjoyment rather than "beating" someone.

Sometimes we include ways to play a game both competitively (with winners and losers) and just for fun. Try both ways—and remember, having a great time is the main objective, and good sports have the most fun!

Get ready to relive a little of your past as you furnish the special young ones in your life with hours of fun and a lifetime of memories. Enjoy!

Adverbally

Type: Guessing and performing
Object: Have fun acting out and guessing words
Players: 3 or more
Ages: 10–adult
Where: Indoors or out
Equipment: Paper, pencils, and a hat, bowl, or basket

An adverb is a word that describes how something is done—for example, *slowly*, *stupidly*, *insanely*. Each player writes down an adverb ending in *ly* on a bit of paper and throws it in a hat, bowl, or basket. Players decide who'll go first, then take turns pulling a word from the hat, bowl, or basket and acting it out. If a player chooses the word he contributed to the hat, that's OK. This possibility discourages players from coming up with words that are too hard to act out!

As a player performs a word (*backwardly*, for instance), all the others try to guess it in a free-for-all manner. To help them, a player may use arms, legs, face, or fingers. He may run, jump, fall, crawl, or whatever it takes to get the guessers to say the adverb. However, a player *may not* use objects, talk, or make sounds.

To make the game competitive, every time a player guesses the word, she earns a letter from the word *ADVERBALLY*. The first correct answer gets an *A*, the next a *D*, and so on. The winner is the first player to get all the letters spelling the entire word.

Alphabet Objects

Type:	Word
Object:	Spot objects starting with the letters *A* through *Z*
Players:	2 or more
Ages:	7 and older; able to read and spell well enough
Where:	On a car trip
Equipment:	None

All the players look out the car windows and try to spot an object that begins with the letter *A*. As soon as a player spots an *A* thing, he calls it out and begins looking for a *B* thing. When one player has named a particular object, no one else may name it, and only that player moves on to the next letter.

The first player to spot an object that starts with every letter of the alphabet, in order, wins. (Players may decide to eliminate the letters *Q*, *X*, and *Z*, or they may require only that objects be spotted that *contain* these letters.)

Anagrams

Type:	Word scrambling
Object:	Unscramble the letters and find the words
Players:	2 or more
Ages:	8 and older; able to read and spell well enough
Where:	On a car trip or anywhere
Equipment:	Paper and pencils

Everyone gets a sheet of paper and a pencil. Each player chooses five words and writes them down—but with the letters all scrambled up. For instance, *table* becomes *letab*, *girl* becomes *igrl*, *upset* becomes *stupe*. Players then trade papers. The first person to unscramble all the words on his or her list wins. Players may decide to limit the length of the words to five or six letters. Also, players should decide whether to allow a solution that is a word but isn't the actual word the scrambler had in mind.

Variation: Players scramble the nouns in a sentence: My sohue has sopchre and nowiwsd. (My house has porches and windows.)

Apple Bobbing

Type: Party
Object: Fish out an apple with mouth
Players: Any number, 1 at a time
Ages: 5 and older; able to put face in water
Where: Outdoors or a waterproofed area
Equipment: A tub, apples, water, towels

This is a popular game for school fairs and backyard barbecues. First, a big tub is filled with water and several apples set loose to float. To bob, a player kneels by the tub with his arms behind his back. Players try to grab an apple. They may use only mouths and teeth—no hands!

Fairs give prizes for snaring an apple. At home, players can take turns competing against the clock for a winner. Whoever snags an apple in the shortest time wins.

Variation: Players can use two tubs and race to snag the apple. Whoever snags the apple first wins. This variation is good for teams, too. To win, each member of the team must snag an apple, in turn, before another team finishes.

Arm Wrestling

Type: Strength contest
Object: Push opponent's arm down
Players: 2
Ages: 4 and older
Where: Seated at a table
Equipment: None

Opponents sit facing one another at a table, elbows on the table, hands clasped palm to palm. Go! Each tries to push her opponent's arm back until the back of her hand touches the table.

To win, a player must push the hand *all the way back* until it touches the table. Arm wrestling is only really fair and fun with two opponents about equal in strength, right-handers against right-handers, and lefties against lefties.

Assassin

Type:	Party
Object:	Catch the Assassin before everyone gets "killed"
Players:	5 or more
Ages:	7 and older
Where:	Around a table or in a circle on the floor or ground
Equipment:	Scrap paper and pencil

Tear or cut a sheet of paper into pieces, one for each player. Mark one piece with an *X*, then fold all pieces over several times. Each player draws a slip and secretly looks to see if the *X* is there. The player who gets the *X* is the Assassin—and no one else must know! The players sit and look at each other, all eyes moving around the circle from face to face, tension rising. To kill a player, the Assassin must make eye contact with the player and then, undetected, wink. The dead player must leave the circle, unless . . .

. . . another player *does* witness the wink. That player will point and shout, "Assassin!" The player who caught the Assassin wins. If the Assassin kills all the players without being caught, the Assassin wins. Rounds are played until one player has five wins—that's the champ!

Backlash

Type:	Race
Object:	Finish first
Players:	4 or more
Ages:	6 and older
Where:	A wide-open area
Equipment:	Air-filled balloons

Players choose a course for the race, either a straight line to a certain spot or a loop. For instance, the course could circle a building. Players pair off (an even number is necessary) and stand back to back with their elbows hooked. With four players, it's a simple pair-versus-pair race. One player in each pair holds a balloon. The pair races halfway around the loop or to the end spot of a straight course. The pair stops and, without unhooking elbows, transfers the balloon to the one in the pair who ran empty-handed, then races on to where they began. First pair back wins.

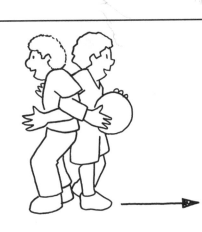

With four, six, or more *pairs* of players, Backlash can be a relay race. Players divide into teams of at least two pairs each. (With large groups with an odd number of players, some players may go twice on one team to even things up.) Each team positions its players at intervals along the course. The pair to run first holds two balloons, one each. When they reach their teammates positioned on the course, they transfer both balloons to the new pair. Pairs must keep their elbows hooked throughout the race!

Once the transfer is complete, the pair continues on. The first team to have its final pair of runners cross the finish line wins!

Bad Sport's Race

Type:	Foot race with tagging
Object:	Be the last one tagged
Players:	4 or more
Ages:	7 and older
Where:	Outdoors, gym
Equipment:	None

First, players mark start and finish lines and side boundaries for a simple foot race. They run the race. The one who loses goes to stand in the middle of the path of the race.

In the next round, the other players race again. This time, the loser of the first round tries to tag the racers. He can tag more than one. Racers can slow down, run circles, whatever it takes to avoid being tagged. But they must stay within the side boundaries and not go back out the starting line.

A tagged player is out of the race and must stand aside. Players keep running rounds until only one runner is left—the winner!

Ball and Caps

Type:	Ball toss and tag
Object:	Throw well and get lowest score
Players:	2 or more
Ages:	8 and older
Where:	Outdoors, gym
Equipment:	A tennis or racquet ball for each player; a cap (or other type of container) for each player

Players place their caps against a wall or the foundation of a house. They stand back a few yards from the wall—far enough to make the game challenging. Players take turns throwing, trying to toss their own balls into someone else's cap.

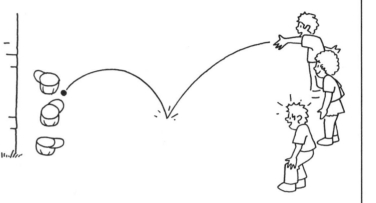

Every time a player throws and misses all the caps, he gets a point. If a player throws the ball into a player's cap, the owner of the cap gets a point (even if it's the thrower's own cap). Because players want the lowest score, this means they should not aim for their own caps! Then the player who threw into a hat runs to the ball. The others scatter. When the thrower has the ball, he yells, "Stop!" Everyone freezes.

The thrower now tosses the ball at a player. (The players must remain still.) If hit, the player gets a point. If not, the thrower gets a point. The players start throwing at the caps again, and play continues until one player reaches the score of 21. The player with the *lowest* score wins.

Ball Duck Race

Type: Relay race with ball
Object: Be first team to complete the race
Players: 4 or more
Ages: 8 and older
Where: Outdoors, gym
Equipment: A similar ball for each team

Players divide into two (or more) teams and mark start and finish lines. The teams line up single file behind the starting line. Each team has one ball. The first in line on each team holds the ball. Go! The team starters race to the finish line.

When they get there, they put the balls between their feet, ankles, or knees and run—er, waddle—back to the starting line as quickly as they can. The next players in line then pick up the balls, run to the far line, and waddle back. The first team to get all its players back and forth wins.

Ball Tag

Type: Tag
Object: Chase and tag opponents with a ball or beanbag
Players: 2 or more
Ages: 5 and older
Where: Outdoors, gym
Equipment: Soft ball or beanbag

As in basic Tag, the player who is It chases the others. To play Ball Tag, It tags not by touching with his hand, but by throwing a soft ball or beanbag. The tagged player is out of the game. The last player to survive is the winner.

Variation: The tagged player becomes It and picks up the ball. Play restarts at once.

13

Ball Volley

Type:	Volleyball-like
Object:	Be first team to score 15 points
Players:	6 or more
Ages:	8 and older; able to catch fairly well
Where:	Outdoors, gym
Equipment:	Rope or net; volleyball or similar type of ball

Players divide a rectangular "court" in two, hang a net or rope in the middle, and divide themselves into two teams. The length of the rope or net and, consequently, the width of the court should be determined by the size, skill, and number of players. This is true also of the placement of the back boundaries (the ones behind the players as they face the net). A member of one team tosses the ball across the net to the opposing team. Someone on the other team catches and returns it. Catching and throwing in this way is called *volleying*.

The teams keep the volley going and take turns serving each time the ball must be served. Players must throw the ball immediately when they catch it. A team may make only one catch and one throw each time the ball comes over to its court. The ball may not touch the ground. If a team drops the ball, hits the net or rope with it, or knocks or drops it out of bounds on its own side, the other team scores a point. If a player throws the ball over the net, but it then goes out of bounds without bouncing or being touched by the other team, the other team gets a point. Play continues until one team has 15 points and is at least 2 points ahead. For instance, if both teams have 14 points, and one team scores, play continues until there is a 2-point difference.

Balloon Duo

Type: Race with balloons
Object: Bat balloon over the finish line first
Players: 4 or more (in pairs)
Ages: 5 and older
Where: Outdoors, gym
Equipment: Air-filled balloons

Players partner up and mark start and finish lines. Partners link arms at the elbow and stand at the start line. One partner holds a balloon.

Go! Players toss the balloon up and, batting the balloon back and forth between them, race to the finish line. If the balloon falls to the ground, they must pick it up and keep going. Runners may not hold or carry their balloons and may not unlink arms. The first pair to bat the balloon over the finish line wins.

Battle at Sea

Type: Paper
Object: Destroy the opponent's navy
Players: 2
Ages: 9 and older
Where: In a car or anywhere
Equipment: Paper and pencils

Players draw grids exactly as shown here. Each player needs two.

Each player draws four ships on her primary grid: one aircraft carrier (four squares blocked off), one cruiser (three squares), and two destroyers (two squares each). The blocks of each ship can be anywhere on the grid, but the blocks of a ship must all touch and be in a line, either horizontally, vertically, or diagonally. Players hide their primary grids from each other during play.

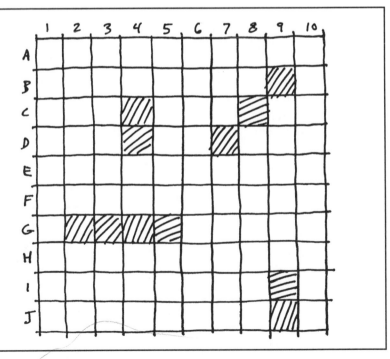

To attack, the first player calls out a letter and number that represent a square on the grid (C-4, for instance). The opponent checks her primary grid. If the attacker's shot hits one of the opponent's ships, the opponent writes an *X* in that square on her primary grid and says, "Hit." If it's not a hit, the opponent says, "Miss." The attacker calls out eleven "shots."

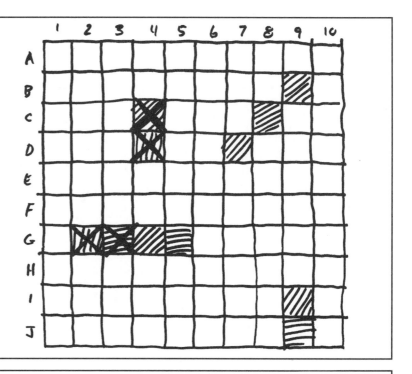

Each time the attacker calls out a number, she listens to the opponent's response (hit or miss) and records it on her second grid. An *X* represents a hit, and a • represents a miss. When the first attacker's eleven shots are used, the opponent takes her eleven shots and records them, just as the first player did. In the next rounds, players get eleven shots *minus the number of hits they suffered in the previous round*. (This is logical; being hit hurts a player's ability to fire.) The goal is to sink all the enemy's ships. To sink a ship, the attacker must hit *all* the blocks of it. The opponent must tell the attacker when a ship gets sunk. The play continues until one player wins by sinking all the ships in the other's navy.

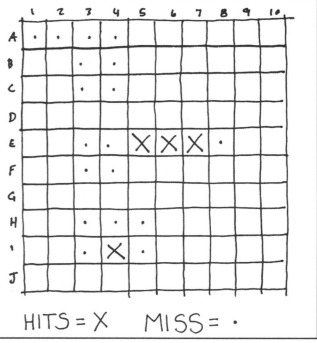

HITS = X   MISS = •

Beanbag Toss

Type: Target tossing
Object: Hit the targets for high score
Players: 2 or more
Ages: 6 and older
Where: Indoors or out
Equipment: Beanbags, one for each player (can be made by filling old socks with dry beans or pebbles), targets (drawn on pavement with chalk or on large sheets of heavy paper, cardboard, or plywood)

Players draw a target (about two and a half feet across) and number the sections. Targets can be as simple as the ones shown here or much more complex. Players establish a throwing line eight, ten, or more feet away. Then they take turns throwing the beanbags, each throwing once, aiming for the sections with high point values. A throw should be scored according to where more of the beanbag lies when it stops. After ten turns, the player with the most points wins. Players also might play until someone wins by reaching a score of 21.

Variation: Players can toss beanbags into numbered targets, such as paper bags, buckets, or pots and pans. The first player to throw into targets 1 to 4 and back wins.

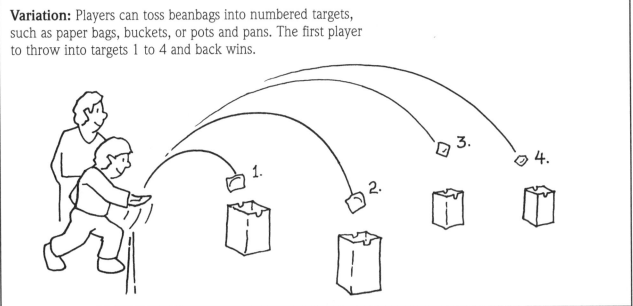

18

Bicycle
Beanbag
Balance

Type: Balance and ride contest
Object: Stay astride the bike with beanbag balanced for the longest time
Players: 2 or more
Ages: Able to ride a bike
Where: A traffic-free, paved or packed-dirt open area
Equipment: Bikes, a beanbag for each player (can be made by filling old socks with dry beans or pebbles)

Riders all balance beanbags on their helmets and get on their bikes. Go! Everyone gets moving. Riders may move any way—in circles, straight, or figure eights—but must not stop. The one who keeps riding *and* keeps the beanbag on his head for the longest time wins.

Variation: Players set up a racecourse with start and finish lines, then run an actual race. If a beanbag falls, that racer is out. First rider across the finish line wins.

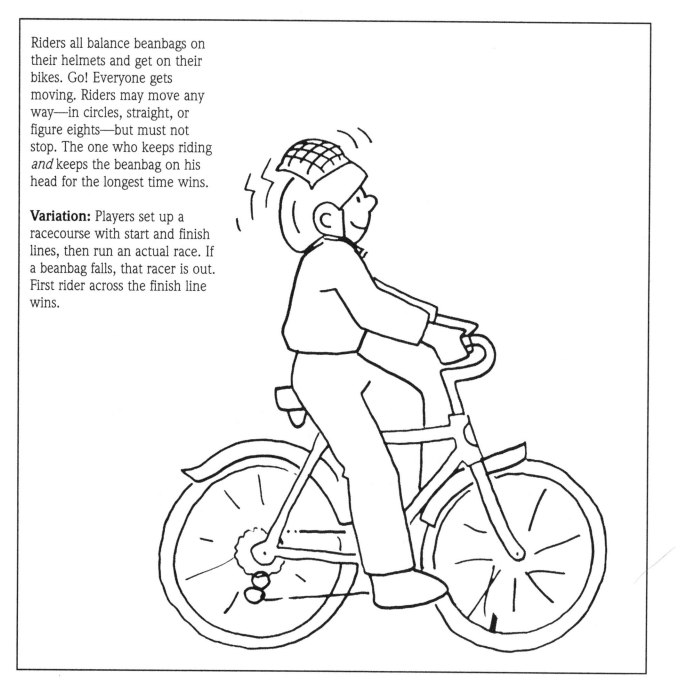

19

Bicycle Coast Race

Type:	Race
Object:	Coast the farthest
Players:	2 or more
Ages:	Able to ride a bike
Where:	A traffic-free, paved or packed-dirt open area
Equipment:	A bike or bikes

Players mark start and finish lines at least thirty feet apart and get on their bikes behind the start line. Go! They pedal as fast as they can from the start to the finish line. At the finish line, riders must stop pedaling and start coasting. The rider who coasts the longest distance is the winner. (If players only have one bike among them, they can simply take turns and mark where they stop.)

Bicycle Slalom Race

Type: Race
Object: Make it through the course first
Players: 2 or more
Ages: Able to ride a bike and time each other using a watch with a second hand
Where: A traffic-free, paved or packed-dirt open area (a long driveway is perfect)
Equipment: Bikes, a dozen or so obstacles (empty milk jugs, buckets, etc.), a stopwatch or a watch with a second hand

Players mark start and finish lines (forty, fifty, or more feet apart) and set obstacles on the course, more or less in a straight line. (The closer together the obstacles, the harder the course will be.) One by one, riders ride from start to finish and must weave in and out around each obstacle. The rider who gets from start to finish the quickest wins. Add one second for an obstacle touched, two seconds for one knocked over, and three for one skipped.

Bicycle Un-Race

Type: Race, in a way
Object: Come in last
Players: 2 or more
Ages: Able to ride a bike
Where: A traffic-free, paved or packed-dirt open area
Equipment: Bikes

A short racecourse—thirty feet or shorter—is fine for this "un-race." Getting there first is *not* the goal! The riders line up at the start. Go! They pedal . . . very . . . slowly . . . toward . . . the finish . . . line. Riders may not touch the ground with their feet, and they must keep going forward. The last one to reach the finish line is the winner.

Bingo

Type: Game of chance
Object: Be first to cover a row of squares
Players: 2 or more
Ages: 6 and older
Where: Anywhere
Equipment: Paper or card paper (whole sheets and cut up pieces), pencils, markers (buttons, pennies, game pieces), 2 bags

Players draw grids (five squares by five squares) with *B I N G O* written across the top, then randomly number the squares with numbers between 1 and 75. No number should appear twice on one card. Players also write the numbers 1 through 75 and the letters *B*, *I*, *N*, *G*, and *O* on the cut-up pieces of card paper, then put the numbers in one bag and the letters in the other. Players take turns removing a number and a letter from the bags, calling them out, then returning them to the bags.

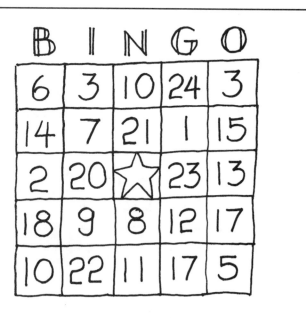

Each time a player's card contains the number called under the letter called, the player covers that square with a marker. (Center square is free—it always counts as covered.) The first player to cover five squares in a row on a card (horizontally, vertically, or diagonally) wins.

Variation: To win, a player must make an X or an L with the markers or cover the entire card.

Bingo for Preschoolers

Type: Game of chance
Object: Be first to cover 6 squares in a row
Players: 2 or more
Ages: 3–5
Where: Anywhere
Equipment: Paper or card paper, crayons, a die, markers (pennies, game pieces, or such)

A grown-up draws the grid shown (including the dice above the grid). Leave the boxes empty, then make copies and color them in—or older preschoolers can do this. Keep the colors simple: yellow, red, green, blue, purple, and orange. Each row should contain only four colors (so two colors will be duplicated, which will speed up the game a little). The players take turns calling out one of the colors—any they choose—then throwing the die. Every time a player's card has a square of the color called under the number on the die thrown, she covers the square with a marker. The first player to cover six squares in a row wins. Rows may be horizontal (across) or vertical (up and down) only.

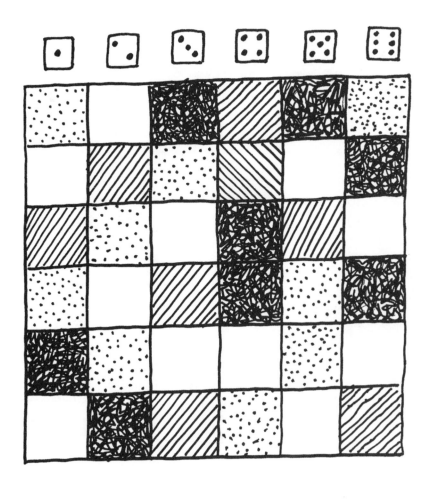

Black Magic

Type: Trick for parties
Object: For tricksters to fool their friends
Players: 6 or more
Ages: 8 and older
Where: Anywhere
Equipment: None

A player claims to be a mind reader and says her friend (John, or whoever) knows it! She says she'll leave the room (or go apart from the group, if outdoors). She tells them to pick an object while she's gone and claims that when she returns, she will read their minds and guess the object. She leaves, they pick an object (the lamp, let's say), and she returns. John, who is in on the trick, starts naming things in the room: "Are we thinking of a jack? A bucket? The lamp? A baseball?" She says, "That's it—the lamp!" How did she know? Because John was using a code! Hours or days before the party, the two of them agreed that the correct object would be the *third one named*. Players may also make up more complex methods. For example, the right object could be the one named after two objects starting with *S* are named. Anything to keep the players baffled!

Variation: If the players catch on (or know the scam already), the mind reader and helper, openly working together, come up with a new code and go through the routine several times. The goal is for the other players to try to figure out the code. Whoever figures it out first gets to choose a partner and be the mind reader.

Blindman's Buff

Type: Tag with a blindfold
Object: Tag opponents while blindfolded
Players: 6 or more
Ages: 5 and older
Where: Outdoors, gym
Equipment: A blindfold

One player, the Blindman, is snugly blindfolded. Everyone else joins hands and walks in a circle around the Blindman. The Blindman claps three times, and the circle stops.

The Blindman points and guesses the name of a player. If the guess is right (unlikely!), the Blindman changes places with that player, who becomes the new Blindman.

But if the guess is wrong, the player steps inside the circle, and the Blindman chases him. When the Blindman tags him, the player must stand still and let the Blindman touch his hair, face, clothes, shoes. The Blindman gets one chance to guess the player's identity. If she guesses right, the other player becomes the Blindman. If she is wrong, the Blindman remains blindfolded and goes another round.

Botticelli

Type: Guessing
Object: Find out who It is thinking of
Players: 2 or more
Ages: 10 and older
Where: On a car trip or anywhere
Equipment: None

This is a game for those who love Jeopardy, Trivial Pursuit, and think the game Virginia Woolf is *way* too easy. In Botticelli, the player who is It thinks of a famous person and announces that person's last initial—let's say *L*, for Abraham Lincoln. The other players take turns asking It questions, trying to get enough information to guess the name. There's no limit to the total number of questions the players may ask. *But* before a player may ask It a real question about the *L* person, the player must ask It a stumper question that It can't answer. The stumper question must be about a person whose name also starts with *L* and must include a clue. Twisted clues make the game more fun! For example, a player asks It, "Who loves a handsome alien?" If It can't guess (Lois Lane), the player then may ask a question about It's *L* person. This must be a yes-or-no question, and It must answer truthfully. (Botticelli, by the way, was an Italian Renaissance painter.)

Warning: not all players feel smart after a round of Botticelli!

Brooklyn Bridge

Type:	Ball rolling
Object:	Eliminate opponents by rolling the ball through their legs
Players:	6 or more
Ages:	5 and older
Where:	Outdoors, gym
Equipment:	Rubber playground ball

Two teams line up and face each other across a space of ten or more feet. Players leave their legs slightly apart, with space about twice the ball's width between their feet. Players should leave a similar amount of space between their own and their teammates' feet. Teams take turns rolling the ball at the opponent's feet. Players are not allowed to move out of the ball's way, but must stay where they are planted!

Once the ball passes between a player's feet, she's out. A team wins by eliminating all its opponents.

Bubble Blow Race

Type: Race, of sorts
Object: Get bubble across the finish line
Players: 2 or more
Ages: 7 and older
Where: Outdoors
Equipment: 1 bowl of bubble liquid and blowing ring for each player or team

Single players may compete, or teams. Players mark start and finish lines about twenty feet apart (longer for team races) and set up one bubble ring and pan of bubble mix for every team or player. The players line up at the start line. Go! Everyone blows the biggest, sturdiest bubble he or she can.

The first player (or team) to blow, fan, or wave a bubble across the finish line wins. Look out—bubbles are unpredictable! If a bubble breaks, the player should stop, blow another one from that spot, and keep going.

Do-It-Yourself Bubble Mix and Blowers
To make really good bubble mix, combine two cups of nonconcentrated dish-washing liquid (we like Dawn), six cups of water, and one cup of corn syrup. To make bubble blowers, remove the ends from empty frozen juice canisters, remove the bottoms of sturdy plastic cups, or form loops with wire clothes hangers.

Cardywinks

Type: Card toss
Object: Bounce card off wall and into hat
Players: 2–4
Ages: 7 and older
Where: Indoors or outdoors
Equipment: Deck or partial deck of cards; hat or cap

Cards are required, but Cardywinks isn't really a card game. Players divide the cards evenly between them and put a hat on the floor against a wall. The players then take turns tossing a card against the wall, trying to get it to bounce into the hat.

If a player misses the hat, the card stays on the ground. If a card goes into the hat without bouncing off the wall first, it stays in the hat. When a player succeeds in bouncing a card off the wall and into the hat, she picks up that card plus all the cards on the floor and in the hat and sets them aside. Play continues until everyone has used up her original stack. Whoever has collected the most cards wins.

Cat and Mouse

Type: Tag
Object: Tag the Mouse
Players: 8 or more
Ages: 4–7
Where: Outdoors, gym
Equipment: None

One player is the Mouse; one is the Cat. All the other players join hands in a circle around the Mouse. When play begins, the Cat is outside the circle, the Mouse in. The Cat tries to tag the Mouse. The Cat may not enter the circle if the players' arms are down.

The Mouse must keep moving, running in and out of the circle. The players holding hands try to help the Mouse, raising their arms to let him in, lowering them to keep the Cat out. When the Cat tags the Mouse, the Mouse becomes the new Cat. The old Cat picks a player to be the Mouse and takes a spot in the circle.

Catch a Cootie

Type: Game of chance
Object: Get silly!
Players: 2 or more
Ages: 7 and older
Where: Anywhere
Equipment: A square sheet of paper and a pencil, pen, or marker for each player

To make a cootie catcher, a player takes a square sheet of paper (a) and folds the corners (b) to the middle (c). Then the player turns the paper over and folds the corners (d) toward the middle and away from the side with the open edges (e).

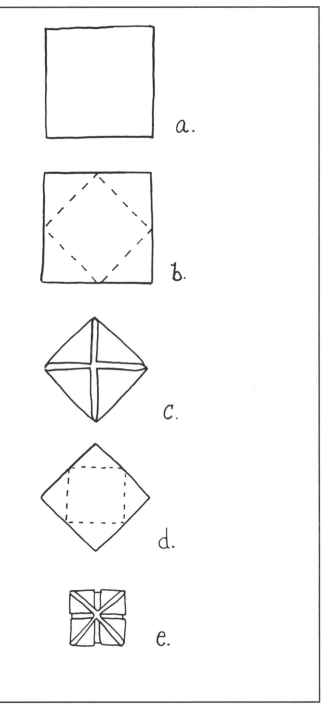

a.

b.

c.

d.

e.

Next, the player creases the catcher so his fingers can go under the flaps (f). With the fingers moving it up and down, the catcher is a kind of mouth that opens vertically and horizontally. The player numbers the eight triangles (two per flap) so that there are two 1s, two 2s, two 3s, and two 4s (g). When the catcher is open one way (or the other), no two like numbers will show at once. The player writes instructions under each number. Under one of the 1s for example, the instruction should be something good: "Have your hair brushed by the other players." Under the other 1, the instruction should be less pleasant: "Kiss everyone's big toe."

Players take turns holding and operating the catcher (h) and take turns choosing a number between 1 and 20. If the person choosing says, "Seven," the operator opens and closes the mouth seven times. The player then chooses a triangle by number, and must do whatever is under that number. It's a gamble—good fortune or bad?

f.

g.

h.

Categories

Type:	Word
Object:	Make the most original list for highest score
Players:	2 or more
Ages:	8 and older
Where:	A car trip or anywhere
Equipment:	Paper and pencils

Players think up twenty categories—anything from states to cars to names of television shows. Each player lists all twenty categories on a sheet of paper. The first player chooses a letter of the alphabet—*N*, for example. Go! Players have five minutes to list something that starts with *N* in each category. Players may skip around the list of categories, but may list only one item under each category until they have at least one item in every category. After that they may add as many items as they can think of in all the categories.

After five minutes, players trade sheets. To score, players take turns reading the lists out loud. As each item is read, the others say whether it appears on their lists. A player scores 2 points for every item she wrote that no other player wrote, 1 point for every item that *was* listed by another player, −1 point for an error (for instance, listing Nebraska under "Countries"), and −1 point for any category with no entries. Each player gets to choose a letter. After each player in the game has had her letter played, players total their scores for all rounds. High score wins.

Caterpillar

Type: Ball passing
Object: Be the first team to cross the finish line
Players: 6 or more
Ages: 6 and older
Where: Outdoors, gym
Equipment: 2 balls of the same kind (beach balls, basketballs, footballs, even balloons)

Players mark start and finish lines fifteen or so feet apart. Two teams line up single file, next to each other, behind the start line. The first person in each line holds a ball.

To begin, the first player in line for each team passes the ball back over her head.

The second player passes it back between his knees, the next back over her head, and so on.

When the ball reaches the last player in line, she runs to the front of her team's line and begins passing the ball back again, over her head. One by one, by running forward when they get the ball, players move their teams toward the finish line. When players go to the front of their line, they may place themselves as far as they please from the player behind. However, if a player drops the ball, the entire team must return to the starting line and begin again. The first team to get all members over the finish line wins.

Chain Story

Type:	Word
Object:	Keep the story going
Players:	3 or more
Ages:	8 and older
Where:	Car trip or anywhere
Equipment:	None

Players decide who'll go first, second, third, and so on. Sitting in a circle or around a table will help; players just take turns clockwise. The first player simply starts telling a story: "Walking through the mall, I saw . . ." As soon as she stops, the next player must quickly continue the story: "a pig riding . . ." Then the next player: "a bicycle. The policeman shouted . . ." Each player finishes a sentence or thought and starts another. Eight words is the limit per turn, and players must end with a verb (an action word). Sometimes stories turn serious, but most often the game dissolves in laughter!

Charades

Type: Guessing
Object: Guess the title
Players: 6 or more
Ages: 10–adult
Where: Usually indoors
Equipment: Paper and pencils

Charades is the grandmother of word and guessing games. To begin, players divide into two teams. The teams go to separate areas to confer privately. Each team chooses a certain number of titles (twice the number of players on the team is good). The titles may be of television shows, plays, movies, books, songs, poems, or even sayings ("A bird in the hand is worth two in the bush"). Teams write each title on a small bit of paper and carefully fold it. Everyone returns to a common room, somewhere big enough for a small "stage" area. Each team puts its titles in a separate hat or bowl. One by one, teams alternating, a player from each team pulls a title from the opposing team's hat. The player must act out the title, and his own teammates try to guess it as quickly as they can. The player acting out a title must follow a few rules. Most important, he may not talk. Also, the player may use no props. (That means, if the word *chair* is in the title, he may not pick up a chair as a clue.) To begin, the player acts out the kind of title:

For a TV show, he draws a square (the TV) in the air.

For a stage play, he pulls a rope, as in raising a theater curtain.

For a movie, he demonstrates holding up a camera and filming.

If it's a book, he holds hands palms together, then opens them, as if opening a book.

If it's a song, he cups his hands to his mouth, as if holding a megaphone.

If it's a saying or quotation, he draws quotation marks in the air.

For a poem, he acts out scribbling.

Next, the player acts out the number of words in the title. If there are five words, he holds up five fingers.

After that, he shows which word he's acting out. If it's the third word, he holds up three fingers.

Next, he shows how many syllables this word has. For three syllables, he holds up three fingers and taps them against his upper arm.

If he's acting out the entire title, he draws a large circle with his hands.

To show that he's acting out something that sounds like (rhymes with) the word, he pulls an ear lobe. Players often use this shortcut when a word itself would be too difficult to act out.

For very small words like *a* or *and* or *the*, he holds two fingers together to indicate something tiny. The others simply guess.

If his teammates' guesses are getting close, he beckons "come here" with his fingers. Players can crawl, cry, pull their hair out. Enthusiasm is more important than acting ability!

In a formal Charades game, players use a watch with a second hand and keep score. A scorekeeper (players can share this job) writes down the length of time each team takes to correctly guess a title. (Three minutes is the limit on trying time.) The team with the shortest total time for all guesses wins. Charades can also be played just for the fun of it. Either way, the laughter and hilarity that break out are the real prize of this game!

Chicken Fights

Type: Pool
Object: Knock opponents off shoulders and into the water
Players: 4 or more (in pairs)
Ages: 8 and older
Where: Outdoors
Equipment: None

Kids have been known to play Chicken Fights on dry land, but this game is easier on the bones in the water! Each pair of partners decides who'll be on top, and that one climbs aboard the other's shoulders. Let the wrestling begin! The player on top pushes, pulls, and bumps until . . .

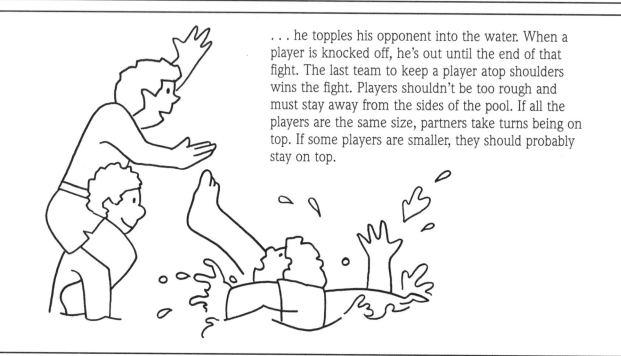

. . . he topples his opponent into the water. When a player is knocked off, he's out until the end of that fight. The last team to keep a player atop shoulders wins the fight. Players shouldn't be too rough and must stay away from the sides of the pool. If all the players are the same size, partners take turns being on top. If some players are smaller, they should probably stay on top.

Cootie-Bug

Type: Drawing
Object: Finish drawing the cootie first
Players: 2 or more
Ages: 5 and older
Where: On a car trip or anywhere
Equipment: Paper, pencils, 1 die

The first player to finish drawing the cootie-bug wins. But players don't just pick up pencils and start drawing. They must roll certain numbers on the die, in a certain order, before drawing the parts of the cootie-bug.

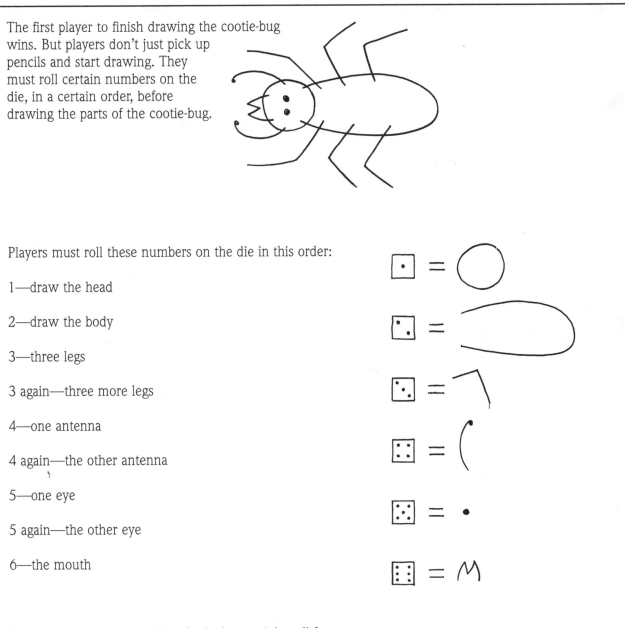

Players must roll these numbers on the die in this order:

1—draw the head

2—draw the body

3—three legs

3 again—three more legs

4—one antenna

4 again—the other antenna

5—one eye

5 again—the other eye

6—the mouth

Players take turns, one roll each. A player might roll for several turns before getting the number she needs. But when she does roll the right number, she gets a free roll.

43

Cracker Race

Type: Messy, crumby, silly
Object: Be first to whistle
Players: 2 or more
Ages: Able to whistle
Where: Anywhere
Equipment: Crackers; broom or Dustbuster

At the same time, all the racers eat the same number of saltine (or other very dry) crackers without drinking. Then everyone tries to whistle "Row, Row, Row Your Boat, Gently Down the Stream." First to whistle that much of the song wins.

Crazy Eights

Type:	Card
Object:	Be first to use all cards
Players:	2–6
Ages:	5 and older
Where:	Car trip or anywhere
Equipment:	Deck of playing cards

The dealer deals seven cards to each player. The dealer then piles the remaining cards facedown on the playing surface (the drawing pile), pulls one card from the drawing pile, and lays it faceup nearby (starting the discard pile). The players arrange their cards and hold them so they can't see each other's cards. The player left of the dealer now must place a card faceup on the discard pile. The card must either be the same number (a two, a king, and so on) or the same suit (spade, heart, diamond, or club) as the card already showing on the discard pile. The exception is that any eight may be discarded at any time. If the player cannot play the right kind card from her hand, she must pull one card from the drawing pile. If she can play that one, she may; if not, her turn is over. The next player goes in the same manner, and the next.

For example, if the top card on the discard pile is the two of clubs, the next player must play either a two . . .

. . . or any club or . . .

. . . any eight. All eights are wild cards. They can be played on any card. Also, when a player plays an eight, she announces the suit (heart, club, spade, or diamond). The next player must play either that suit or another eight. If a player does not have the needed card, she draws a card from the pile. First one to play all her cards wins.

Variation: When a player does not have the suit or number to play a card on her turn, she draws from the pile and keeps drawing until she pulls a card she can use.

Cross Tag

Type:	Tag
Object:	Tag the others
Players:	3 or more
Ages:	5 and older
Where:	Outdoors, gym
Equipment:	None

As in basic Tag, It chases and tries to tag the others. With Cross Tag, though, all the players work together to defeat It. First, It calls out the name of one of the players. It takes off after that player, and all the others begin running around. It may chase *only* the named player unless . . .

. . . another player passes between them. . . .

. . . Then It must chase that player, until yet another player passes between It and the chased one, and so on. All the players join in to help distract and confuse It. When a player is tagged, she's the new It. The new It calls out a name, and play begins again.

Deadly Queen

Type:	Cards
Object:	Run out of cards and not end up with the deadly queen
Players:	3–6
Ages:	5 and older (small hands may need help holding the cards)
Where:	Anywhere
Equipment:	Deck of cards

The dealer removes all the queens from the deck except the queen of spades, then deals out all the cards. First, players examine their cards. They remove any pairs (two of the same number or face type, whether black or red) they have and lay them all together, faceup on the table. Players hold their remaining cards so they can't see each other's cards. Someone has the queen!

The player on the dealer's left then pulls one card at random from the dealer's hand. If that card matches one in his own hand, he lays both of them on the table with the others. If not, he keeps it. The player to his left now pulls from the first player's hand, and so on, around the table. In this way, players slowly empty their hands—and the queen moves around the table. In the end, all the card pairs will be laid down, and someone ends up with the queen. That player is the big loser!

Dodge War

Type:	Ball tag
Object:	Tag opponent out
Players:	8 or more
Ages:	6 and older
Where:	Outdoors, gym
Equipment:	Rubber playground ball

Mark off a large rectangle. For two teams of four or five players each, eighteen- by twenty-foot sides will do. Use longer sides for bigger teams. Each team numbers its players consecutively (one through whatever) and chooses a player to be the first caller. If one team has five members and the other has six, the fifth member on the smaller team can be Five *and* Six. Someone places the ball in the center of the rectangle. The team members line up, in order, along opposite sides. The caller (teams take turns) shouts a number: "Three!" The two Threes (one from each team) run to the ball. The Three who gets to the ball first picks it up and stops where he is. The other Three backs off as far as possible within the rectangle.

Before the ball holder can throw and try to tag the other Three, he must count to ten out loud. Without moving, he then has one try to hit the other Three. If he hits him, the thrower's team scores a point. If not, both players go back to their places, and the game starts over. The winning team is the first to score 21 points.

Dodgeball

Type:	Ball tag
Object:	Tag players out with the ball
Players:	7 or more
Ages:	7 and older
Where:	Outdoors, gym
Equipment:	A rubber playground ball

Players draw a circle on pavement or mark one in grass. Everyone stands along the circle except It, who stands in the center. The players throw the ball back and forth across the circle, trying to tag It. It stays in the center as long as she can avoid getting hit. (If It seems to get hit immediately, the circle is too small. If hitting It seems impossible, the circle should be smaller.) The player who hits It gets a point and names a new It. (The player with the most points is a good choice!) The old It rejoins the circle. The first player to have 5 points wins.

Dodgeball Reverse

Type:	Ball tag
Object:	Avoid being tagged with the ball
Players:	5 or more
Ages:	6 and older
Where:	Outdoors, gym
Equipment:	A rubber playground ball

Each player chooses a color (a different color for each player). All the players except one stand in two rows. The remaining player stands in the middle, holding the ball. One player is the caller for each round. (Players take turns.) The caller shouts a color: "Green!" The player who chose that color runs across the space. The middle player throws the ball, trying to tag the runner with it before the runner reaches the other line.

If the runner is hit, he gets a point and becomes the ball thrower.

But if the thrower misses the runner, the thrower stays put for the next round. Either way, the next caller shouts a color, and a new runner goes. Every time a runner gets hit, she gets a point. Play continues until only one player has no score. That player wins!

With large groups, more than one player can have the same color. When a color is called, all the players who chose that color run at the same time. In the unlikely event that two runners are tagged on the same throw, use Scissors, Paper, Stone to determine who becomes the thrower. Each gets a point.

Variation: Players can use numbers, states, or even superheroes instead of colors.

Drop Dead

Type: Game of chance
Object: Get high score on the dice
Players: 2 or more
Ages: 7 and older
Where: Anywhere
Equipment: 5 dice; pencil and paper for score keeping

In each round each player has one turn, in which he or she throws the dice a number of times. The first player throws all five dice and adds up the dots showing for the score.

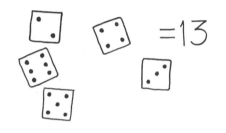

However, any 5 or 2 rolled is worth no points. Throwing a 2 or 5 on the dice is unlucky in this game.

Before throwing again, the player must set aside the 5 and the 2. The player then throws the remaining three dice and adds them up.

$=12$

Before the next throw, the player again removes any 2s or 5s. The player throws again, adds, . . .

$=4$

. . . throws again, removes 2s or 5s, adds, and continues.

$=3$

One turn lasts until all the dice have landed on 2 and 5 and have been eliminated. A game consists of three rounds (one turn each, with many throws, per player). High score wins.

$0 =$

52

Drop the Hankie

Type:	Race
Object:	Beat It around the circle
Players:	7 or more
Ages:	4 and older
Where:	Outdoors, gym
Equipment:	A hankie, tissue, or some such item

Everybody except It stands in a circle, holding hands. It walks or runs around the outside of the circle, holding a hankie.

Without pausing, It drops the handkerchief behind a player. Players should be alert!

When It drops the hankie behind a player, the player must pick it up and race It around the circle.

Whoever gets back to the opening in the circle first is safe. The other one is the next It.

Duck, Duck, Goose

Type: Race and chase
Object: Outrun the Goose
Players: 8 or more
Ages: 5 and older
Where: Indoors or outdoors
Equipment: None

Everyone except It sits in a circle. It walks around the outside of the circle, behind the players' backs. It taps gently on the players' heads and says, "Duck . . . Duck . . . ." But on one player's head, . . .

. . . It taps, says, "Goose!" and starts running. The Goose jumps up and chases It around the circle.

If the Goose doesn't tag It before It reaches her spot in the circle, It takes her place in the circle. The Goose becomes the new It. If the Goose does tag It, she gets back in the circle and It is It again.

Egg or Water-Balloon Toss

Type: Tossing competition
Object: Toss the farthest while keeping the egg or balloon intact
Players: 2 or more teams of 2
Ages: 6 and older
Where: Outdoors!
Equipment: Uncooked eggs or balloons filled with water

Each team of two has a raw egg (or water-filled balloon). The partners face each other, about arm's length apart. The two partners begin carefully tossing the egg or balloon between them. Each time it survives the toss without breaking, both take a step back and toss again.

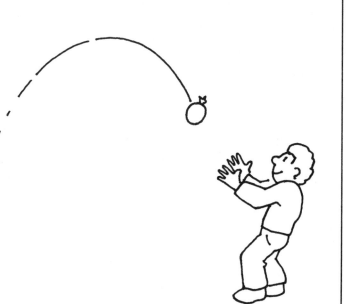

The winner is the team that can step back the farthest and throw without breaking the egg (or bursting the balloon).

Egg Polo

Type:	Blowing contest
Object:	Blow egg over the opponent's goal line
Players:	2
Ages:	4 and older
Where:	Indoors or out
Equipment:	Whole raw egg

Players place a hollow eggshell (see below) exactly in the middle of a tabletop, then stand across the table from each other. The table edges where they are standing are the goal lines. The object is simple: Each player tries to blow the egg over the opponent's goal line and score a point. Players may only *blow*; they may not use their hands. Also, if one player blows the egg over a side edge, the other player gets the point. After every point, players replace the egg in the middle and go again. First player to score 5 points wins.

Hollowing Out an Eggshell
To hollow out an eggshell, use a small knitting needle (or similar tool) to carefully make two small holes on opposite ends of a raw egg. Gently blow into one hole, over a bowl, forcing the egg out. (Refrigerate the egg, but cook it soon!) Ping-Pong balls also work, but the irregular roll of an egg does add to the fun!

Exquisite Corpse

Type:	Drawing
Object:	Just plain fun
Players:	3 or more
Ages:	8 and older
Where:	A car trip or anywhere
Equipment:	Paper and pencils

Some artists in the 1930s used Exquisite Corpse to create serious art. It's good for just plain fun, too. Each player has a pencil and a sheet of paper, which she folds in three.

Each player draws a head on the top section of her sheet, folds it so only the blank midsection shows, and passes it along to the player to the right.

Next, each player draws a body on the midsection of the sheet handed to her, and passes right again.

Finally, each player draws feet on the bottom section of the third sheet handed to her. Each time players hand a sheet to the right, they show only the blank next section to the new drawer, so that . . .

. . . what they see when they open the sheets is quite bizarre!

Farmer, Farmer, May We Cross?

Type: Tag
Object: Avoid getting tagged by the Farmer
Players: 5 or more
Ages: 5 and older
Where: Outdoors, gym
Equipment: None

One player is the Farmer. The Farmer stands in the middle of a long open space. The other players line up together on one side. The lined-up players call out, "Farmer, Farmer, may we cross your field?" The Farmer chooses a color and calls out, "Only if you're wearing *Blue*!"

Any player wearing blue (blue anything—a ring, handkerchief, blouse, whatever) may cross over safely. When all the Blues are safe, . . .

. . . those who aren't wearing blue must make a mad dash. The Farmer tags as many of them as he can.

Any player tagged by the Farmer must sit out. The remaining players repeat the game, with the Farmer choosing different colors, until the last player is caught. That player wins.

Follow-Up Goal

Type:	Pickup basketball
Object:	Score points by making baskets
Players:	2
Ages:	6 and older
Where:	A basketball court
Equipment:	Basketball hoop and ball

The first player shoots from the free throw line. Players may use the one on the court (if there is one) or establish one to suit themselves. The other player stands near the basket. If the first player makes the shot, . . .

. . . she gets a point and another free throw. She keeps taking shots from the free throw line, getting a point for every basket she makes, until . . .

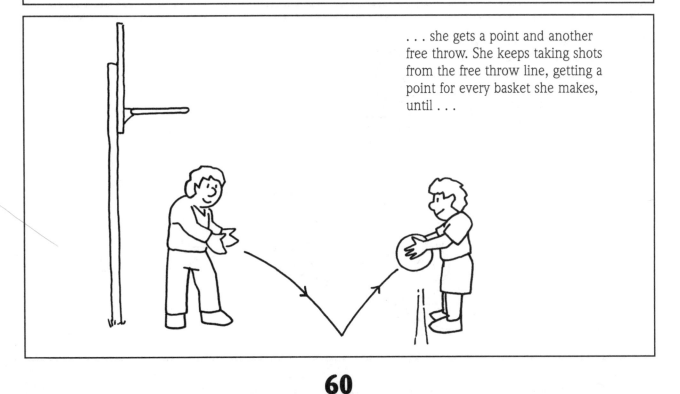

. . . she misses. Then she moves to the basket. If she can catch the rebound before it bounces, she may . . .

. . . *immediately* shoot from under the basket (a layup). If she makes the layup, she gets a point. Either way, her turn is now over, and the other player takes a turn. After they each take ten turns, the player with the highest total score wins.

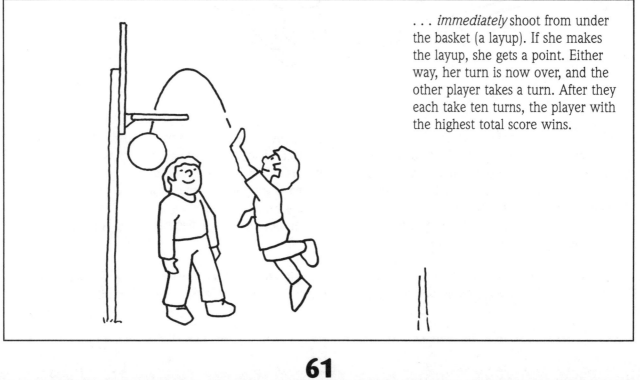

Four Square

Type: Handball in a square court
Object: Hit the ball accurately for low score
Players: 4–7
Ages: 8 and older
Where: Outdoors, gym
Equipment: Tennis or racquet ball (the bouncier the ball, the harder the game)

Players draw a square court and divide it into four squares. A player stands in each square. One player serves into any other square. To do this, she bounces the ball once in her square, then hits it to another square. The person in that square must hit the ball after it bounces, delivering it to another square. In this way, the players volley: hit, bounce, hit, bounce. Players get points in one of three ways: for hitting a ball out of the court instead of into a square; for hitting a ball so it lands on a line; or for failing to hit the ball after it has bounced one time in her square. When one player reaches a score of 10, the game's over. The player with the lowest score wins.

Variations: With more than four players, kids can rotate in and out after every serve, each one staying in for exactly four serves. After everyone has rotated in twice, the player with the lowest score wins.

Fox and Hen

Type: Chase
Object: For the Fox, to catch Chicks; for the Chicks, to keep from being caught
Players: 5 or more
Ages: 4 and older
Where: Outdoors, gym
Equipment: None

One player is the Fox, one the Hen. The other players are Chicks. The Chicks line up behind the Hen, forming a chain by holding each other's hands. The Fox crouches, and the Hen and Chicks circle at a good distance, with the Hen staying between the Fox and her Chicks. The Chicks start teasing the Fox:

CHICKS: What are you doing, Fox?

FOX: Picking up sticks.

CHICKS: Why?

FOX: To build a fire.

CHICKS: Why?

FOX: To cook dinner.

CHICKS: What's for dinner?

FOX: [*Leaps up and yells*] Chicken!

The Fox goes after the last Chick in line. To protect her Chick, the Hen tries to keep facing the Fox. This makes her whip the Chicks around behind her. When the Fox captures a Chick, the Fox becomes the Hen, and the caught Chick is the new Fox.

Freeze Tag

Type: Tag
Object: Chase and tag the others
Players: 4 or more
Ages: 4 and older
Where: Outdoors, gym
Equipment: None

As in basic Tag, It chases and tries to tag the others. But in Freeze Tag, when a player gets tagged, he must hold absolutely still . . .

. . . until "unfrozen" by the tag of another player.

It will have difficulty freezing all the players; they all keep unfreezing each other! But if she does, she gets to choose the next It.

Frisbee Golf

Type: Frisbee target shooting
Object: Hit all targets with the fewest tries
Players: 2–7
Ages: 7 and older
Where: Outdoors, in a large space such as a playground or lightly wooded area
Equipment: A Frisbee (2 or more make the game go faster); paper and pencil for score keeping

Players choose some objects for targets—barrels, swing sets, bushes, doghouses, and so on—and decide the order in which to shoot for them. The distance between targets, and between the starting spot and first target, should depend on the skill of the players. To start, one player aims for the first target. If he doesn't hit the target the first time, he takes another try from where the Frisbee fell, and another, until he hits the target. Every try earns him a point.

Next, the rest of the players take turns shooting for the same target. Each player takes as many tries as needed, each time trying from where the Frisbee landed. The player gets a point for every try.

When all players have hit the first target, they record their scores. Then they move on to the second target, shooting one by one, then to the third, and so on. At the end of the course, the player with the lowest score wins.

Fruit Basket

Type: Seat switch
Object: Avoid getting left without a seat
Players: 6 or more
Ages: 5 and older
Where: Outdoors, gym
Equipment: None

The players sit in a circle, a foot or two apart. Before play starts, they mark the seating spots. They can make *X*s with chalk or, on grass, use markers such as leaves or brown paper bags. These seats are the only place players may sit to be safe. Each player chooses a different fruit out loud. Players choose an It, who sits in the middle and starts telling a story. Eventually, the fruits must enter into the story, two at a time—for instance, "I saw on the kitchen table some bananas and apples . . ."

At once, those whose fruits were named—the apple player and the banana player—jump up. They must change places. But It jumps up, too, and will try to get one of their seats.

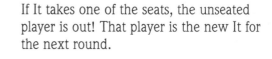

If It takes one of the seats, the unseated player is out! That player is the new It for the next round.

Variation: With large groups (twelve kids or more), let two players share each fruit.

German

Type: Handball
Object: Hit the ball to score points
Players: 4–8
Ages: 8 and older
Where: Outdoors, gym, with a wall to play against
Equipment: Chalk and soft, small, bouncy ball

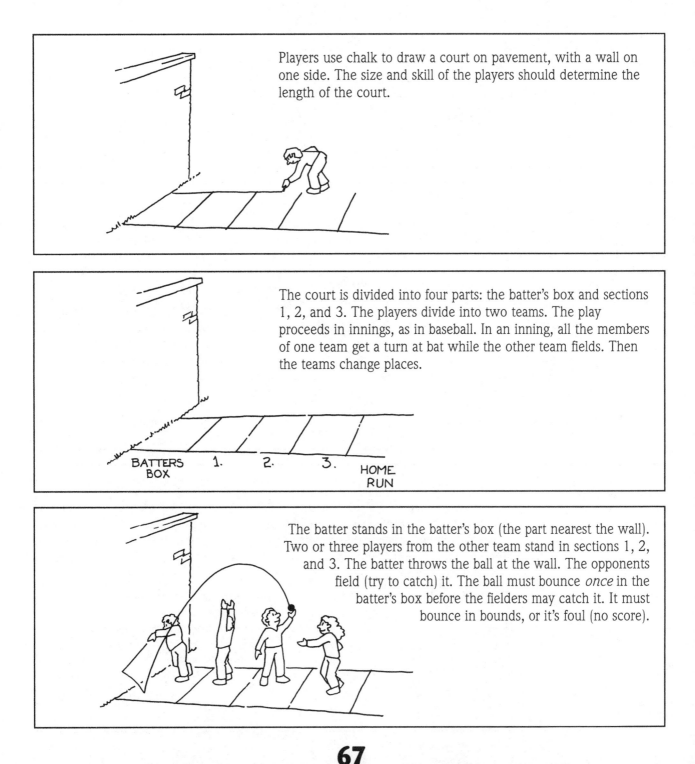

Players use chalk to draw a court on pavement, with a wall on one side. The size and skill of the players should determine the length of the court.

The court is divided into four parts: the batter's box and sections 1, 2, and 3. The players divide into two teams. The play proceeds in innings, as in baseball. In an inning, all the members of one team get a turn at bat while the other team fields. Then the teams change places.

BATTERS BOX   1.   2.   3.   HOME RUN

The batter stands in the batter's box (the part nearest the wall). Two or three players from the other team stand in sections 1, 2, and 3. The batter throws the ball at the wall. The opponents field (try to catch) it. The ball must bounce *once* in the batter's box before the fielders may catch it. It must bounce in bounds, or it's foul (no score).

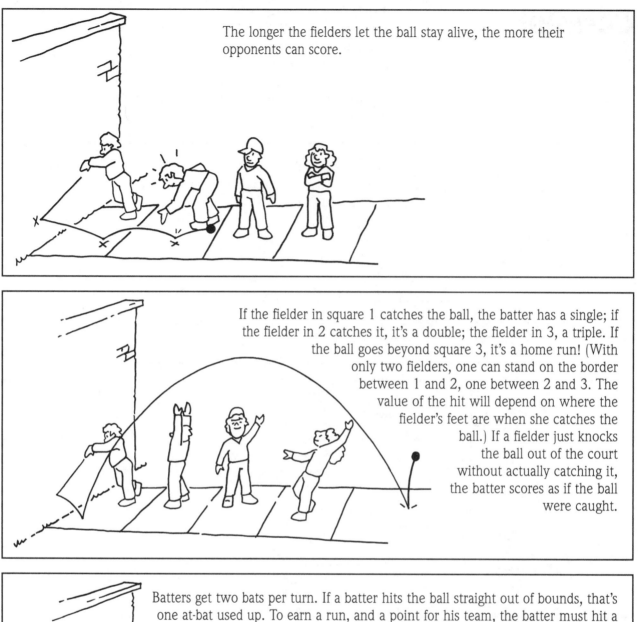

The longer the fielders let the ball stay alive, the more their opponents can score.

If the fielder in square 1 catches the ball, the batter has a single; if the fielder in 2 catches it, it's a double; the fielder in 3, a triple. If the ball goes beyond square 3, it's a home run! (With only two fielders, one can stand on the border between 1 and 2, one between 2 and 3. The value of the hit will depend on where the fielder's feet are when she catches the ball.) If a fielder just knocks the ball out of the court without actually catching it, the batter scores as if the ball were caught.

Batters get two bats per turn. If a batter hits the ball straight out of bounds, that's one at-bat used up. To earn a run, and a point for his team, the batter must hit a home run or two doubles or a single plus a triple or a double plus a triple. If he makes only two singles, they still may not be wasted. All the team's hits in the inning may be combined to earn runs. If the team's next batter hits a double or better, it is combined with the first batter's singles to add up to a run. (This is similar to how runners advance in baseball.)

If a team has some leftover hits at the end of the inning (that don't add up to a run), these hits *do not* carry over to the next inning. After five innings, the team with the most runs wins.

German Singles

Type: Handball
Object: Hit the ball well to score points
Players: 2
Ages: 8 and older
Where: Outdoors, gym, with a wall to play against
Equipment: Chalk and soft, small bouncy ball

Draw the same kind of court as for German. The players take turns being the batter. The batter throws the ball against the wall; it must bounce first into the batter's box. Then the fielder tries to stop it by catching or deflecting it. If he stops it before its second bounce, no score. If the batter hits the ball out the sides, it's foul, and there's no score. If the fielder fails to stop the ball after its first bounce, the batter gets the score from whatever box the ball next lands in: first box, 1 point; second box, 2 points; third, 3 points; beyond that, 4 points. Each batter gets five tries per inning. High score after five innings wins.

Goal Kickers

Type:	Soccer-like court game
Object:	Kick the ball over the opponent's goal to score
Players:	6 or more
Ages:	8 and older
Where:	Outdoors, gym
Equipment:	Soccer ball or rubber playground ball

Teams take sides in a divided, rectangular court. For eight players, a twenty- by forty-foot court is about right. For fewer players, a smaller court is better. Play starts with a tip-off. To tip off, one player from each team stands at the center line. Another player (teams take turns choosing one) tosses the ball up between the players. The two players jump up and try to tap the ball into their side of the court. (Players may not score on the tip-off.) The tip-off is the only time players may use their hands. For the rest of the play, they move the ball only with their feet.

After the tip-off, the players begin kicking the ball back and forth between the two sides of the court. The object is for the players to kick the ball between the opposing team members and out the back boundary, which is the goal line. When the ball comes to a player, he may stop it with his body and feet as it comes to him and line up a shot. Or he may just kick or knee it as soon as it reaches him.

A player may use any part of his body—except his hands—to try to stop the ball, knock it out of bounds, or score. There is no limit to how many times a team or player may bump the ball while it's on their side.

If a player kicks the ball past the goal line, he scores a point for his team. The teams tip off again after each score and when the ball goes out of bounds. The team that first scores 21 points wins.

Variation: Play on the clock. Whoever is ahead after ten minutes wins.

Grab Tag

Type: Tag
Object: For It to tag the others
Players: 2 or more
Ages: 5 and older
Where: Outdoors, gym
Equipment: None

In this version of Tag, It chases and tries to tag the other players. When tagged, a player becomes It, but that's not all.

The tagged player also must grab his tagged spot—whether a shoulder, elbow, or knee—and hold it while he goes after the others. So, the player who is It shouldn't just try to tag players, but try to tag them in the most awkward place possible!

Greedy

Type: Pickup basketball
Object: Score the most points by making the most baskets
Players: 2 or more
Ages: 8 and older
Where: A formal or informal basketball court
Equipment: A basketball for each player

Each player holds a ball and stands the same distance from the basket. On your mark, get set, go! Everybody shoots! Over and over and over, they shoot, scoring as many baskets as possible.

If a player loses control of her ball, she runs after it and gets back to shooting as fast as she can. The first player to build up 10 points wins.

Variation: Players compete against the clock. The winner is the player who has the most points after five (or ten) minutes.

Greek Ball

Type: Ball throwing
Object: Throw ball over the other team's boundary to score
Players: 10 or more
Ages: 7 and older
Where: Outdoors, gym
Equipment: Rubber playground ball or soccer ball

Players divide into two teams and set boundary lines fifteen feet apart or more, depending on the age and skill of the players. Teams line up on opposing boundary lines, with each team's players standing several feet apart from one another. The ball is placed in the middle.

To start, one runner from each team dashes to the ball, trying to pick it up first. As the game progresses, members of a team take turns making the dash. Opponents should run from directly opposite one another, so that they are an equal distance from the ball.

The player who gets the ball tries to throw it over the other team's line. The defending players may stop the ball by catching, bumping, or deflecting it. If they stop the ball, the runners return to their lines, and someone puts the ball back in the center for the next runners. If they don't stop the ball and it goes over the line, the thrower's team gets a point, then the next runners try. Play continues until one team reaches a score of 21. That team wins.

Hand Tennis

Type: Small ball volleying
Object: Volley the ball accurately to score
Players: 4 or more
Ages: 9 and older
Where: Outdoors, gym
Equipment: Soft bouncy ball

Players draw a court on pavement and divide it into two. For eight players (four on each team), twenty by forty feet should be about right. For fewer players, the court should be smaller. Each team takes one side of the court and picks a player to serve first. The players spread out so that they each have an informal area of responsibility for the ball. They may shift positions occasionally, giving players a chance to play different parts of the court. The server should be one of the players on the back of the court.

(Teams take turns serving.) The server simply tosses the ball underhand into the other team's side. The served ball must go straight into the opponents' court. Once it's there, the other team tries to bat it back, after or before it bounces. The ball may bounce more than once in a court before the team returns it. As long as the ball keeps bouncing and stays in the court, the volley continues.

If a team fails to return the ball, scoring depends on where the ball lands. If the ball dies (stops bouncing) inside a team's court, the other team scores a point. If the ball goes out the back boundary of a team's court, the other team scores a point. If a team knocks the ball out the sidelines of its own court, or out the sidelines of the opponents' court without it first bouncing in the team's own court, there is no score. The ball goes to the other team, which serves it.

Play continues until one team wins by scoring 21 points. A 2-point lead is necessary to win.

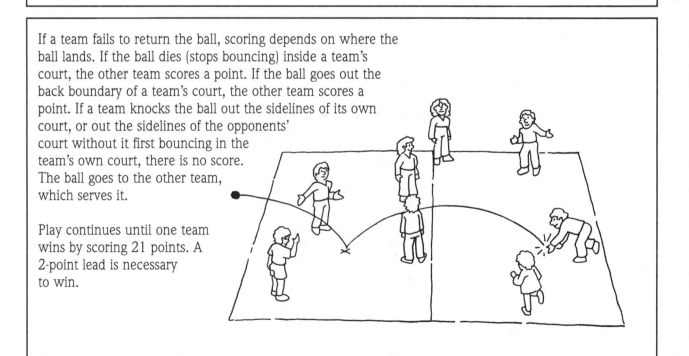

Hand Wrestling

Type: Test of strength
Object: Overpower the opponent
Players: 2, roughly equal in size and strength
Ages: 7 and older
Where: Indoors or out
Equipment: None

Two opponents stand facing each other with their right (or left) feet together heel to toe. They brace themselves, plant their feet firmly, and clasp hands. Go! Both players put all their strength into trying to unbalance the opponent.

The first player to lose his balance to the point where he stumbles or takes a step loses.

Variation: For rougher action, the players wrestle until one of them touches some body part other than a foot (knee, leg, or bottom) to the ground.

Handball

Type: Ball hitting and volleying with hands
Object: Win the volley and score
Players: 2 or 4
Ages: 10 and older
Where: Outdoors, gym
Equipment: Chalk and handball, racquet ball, or tennis ball

Regulation handball courts in gyms and health clubs use all four walls and the floor and ceiling in play. But all that's really necessary for two (or four) players to have fun is the simple court shown here, which can be chalked on a paved surface up against a wall. Players may size it to suit themselves. In handball, the players serve against the wall, then try to keep the volley going. During the volley it's OK for players to move outside the court so long as, when they hit the ball, it stays within the court.

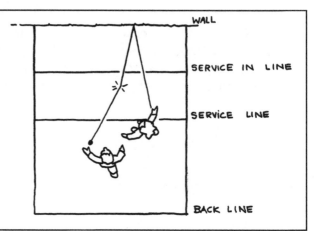

To serve, the player stands inside the sidelines and between the service in line and the service line. The server throws the ball straight down in a controlled way, so it will bounce straight up. When it comes up, the server hits the ball with an open hand against the wall.

The receiving player, also standing behind the serving line, tries to hit the ball against the wall so that it bounces back into the court and not out of bounds. The volley keeps going until somebody misses or makes an error.

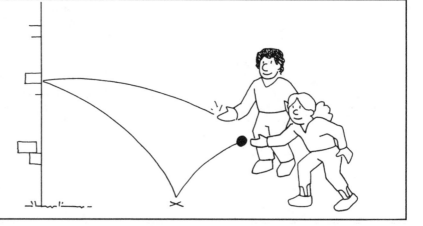

In Handball, only the player who served can score on a particular ball. Therefore, it is important for players to keep track of whose serve it is. If a player serves, and the other player misses during the following volley, the server scores and then serves again. But if a player serves and then misses or makes an error during the following volley, there's no score. His serve is over, and the other player begins to serve.

The serving player gets a second chance to serve when:

• The first serve doesn't make it past the service line. (This is called a *short ball*.)
• The first serve goes past the back line. (This is a *long ball*.)
• The first serve hits her opponent.

But if the first and second serves do any two of these things, the serve is over.

A server does not get a second try to serve if:

• The serve hits a side line.
• Her serve hits her (or her partner, in doubles).

Doubles

In doubles, four players play at one time, as partners. The server's partner stands outside the sidelines during the serve. The partner only comes into the court after the ball has been served and bounced past the service line. In doubles, players must be especially careful to stay out of the way of any player trying to hit the ball. Doubles may be played either so that the partners take turns hitting the ball when it's their team's turn to hit it, OR that whatever partner is closest to the ball hits it.

Note: Players must get out of each other's way when they are playing. If it's one player's turn to hit the ball, the other must not block or hinder her. Play continues until one player has 15 points (or 21). A player must win by at least 2 points.

Hangman

Type: Word
Object: Figure out a secret word
Players: 2
Ages: 8 and older; able to read well enough
Where: On a car trip or anywhere
Equipment: Paper and pencil

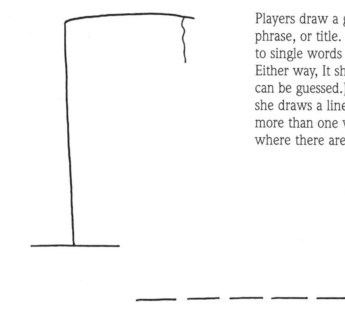

Players draw a gallows as shown. It chooses a word, phrase, or title. (Players may choose to limit the game to single words or to titles of books, songs, or movies. Either way, It should be fair and choose something that can be guessed.) When It has chosen a word or phrase, she draws a line of dashes, one for every letter. With more than one word, It should leave obvious spaces where there are spaces between words.

The other player tries to guess It's word, one letter at a time. If the player guesses a letter correctly, It prints it on the correct dash. Each time the player guesses a letter *not* contained in It's word, It jots the letter down elsewhere on the page and adds a part to a stick figure suspended from the gallows. For every wrong guess, the stick figure gets a head, trunk, arm, arm, leg, leg, foot, foot (in that order). To make the game easier, players may also allow adding toes and fingers, eyes, nose, and mouth.

H O _ _ E

A, I, U, M

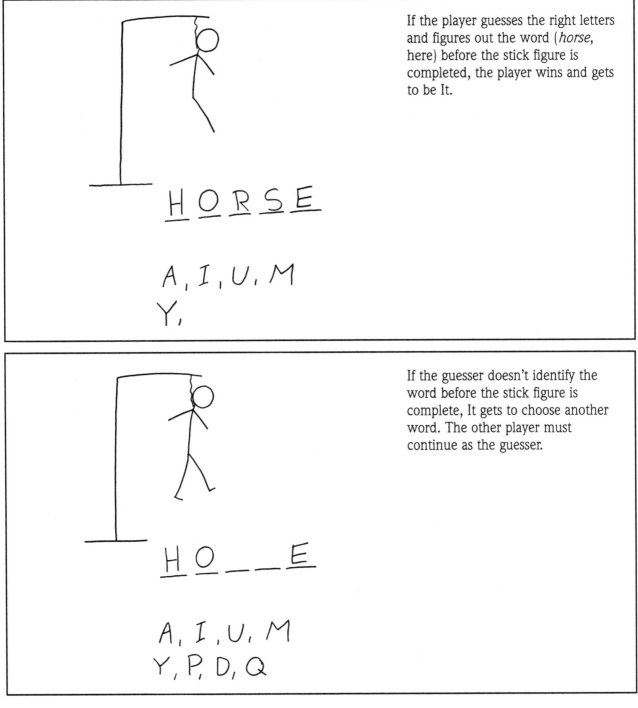

If the player guesses the right letters and figures out the word (*horse*, here) before the stick figure is completed, the player wins and gets to be It.

If the guesser doesn't identify the word before the stick figure is complete, It gets to choose another word. The other player must continue as the guesser.

Hat Thieves

Type: Grab and tag
Object: Get the hat out of bounds without getting tagged
Players: 6 or more
Ages: 7 and older
Where: Outdoors, gym
Equipment: A hat, shoe, beanbag, or other object to grab

The players divide into two teams (the Thieves and the Guards). They mark a playing area twenty or more feet square and put a hat in the center of the square. Teams stand opposite each other, outside the borders. One team chooses a Guard to go first; the other team chooses a Thief. When the Guard is ready, he steps in. That's the signal for the Thief to go after the hat, trying to grab it and carry it out of bounds. A Thief can rarely just get there first, grab the hat, and go. Thief and Guard usually get there at about the same time. They circle the hat. The Thief makes fake grabs, trying to fool the Guard. What happens next determines whether the Thief or the Guard scores for his team.

The Thief will score a point if the Guard touches the Thief in any way before the Thief steals the hat, or if the Guard touches the hat in any way while it's still on the ground.

The Thief also will score a point if he gets the hat out of bounds without being tagged.

The Guard will score a point if he tags the Thief after the Thief has the hat. After each round, teams alternate sending out Guards and Thieves. Play continues until one team wins by scoring 11 points.

Variation: Play continues by elimination. In elimination play, when a player—Thief or Guard—is scored against, she is out. When all the members of a team have been eliminated, the other team wins.

Hide-and-Seek

Type: Hiding
Object: Hide and don't get found
Players: 3 or more
Ages: 3 and older
Where: Best outdoors; possible in a big house
Equipment: None

It closes his eyes (or is blindfolded or faces a wall) and counts out loud (to fifty or one hundred; for preschoolers, a slow count to ten) while the others hide. If playing outdoors, players should decide beforehand on boundaries and hide inside those boundaries.

It finishes counting and starts searching for the other players.

The first player It finds is the new It. It yells, "Allie, Allie, in come free!" All players come out of their hiding places.

Variation: If there are many players, It does not stop searching after finding one hider, but must continue until he finds them all. The last player discovered is the winner and gets to name the new It.

Hide-and-Seek and Go Home

Type:	Hiding
Object:	Hide and race back home
Players:	3 or more
Ages:	4 and older
Where:	Best outdoors; possible in a big house
Equipment:	None

It hides his face and counts out loud (to fifty or one hundred, or for young players, a slow count to ten or twenty). The place where It counts is Home. The others hide while It is counting. Outdoors, players decide beforehand on boundaries and hide inside the boundaries.

It finishes counting and starts searching for the other players.

Unlike in basic Hide-and-Seek, players don't find a hiding place and stay there. When It is not looking in their direction, hiders try to run Home. Players may run for Home anytime they want, but they *must* run there once It spots them. It tries to tag players as they run Home. A player who gets Home without being tagged stays there and is safe.

The game is over as soon as It tags a player. The tagged player becomes It. If all the players get home safely, the same person is It.

Variation: Play continues until every player has either run Home or been tagged. The last one to be tagged is It—which makes all the players want to get home early! If one player hides in an unfindable spot, It may give up and call, "Allie, Allie, in come free!" Any remaining hiders can come out and be safe; It has been defeated and must be It again.

Hide the Button

Type: Search
Object: Find the hidden button
Players: 3 or many more
Ages: 4 and older
Where: Usually indoors
Equipment: A small object to hide

In this rainy day pastime, It stays alone in a room while all the other players leave. Somewhere in the room, It hides a small button (or penny or stone). The button may show slightly or be completely hidden. It then calls the other players back in.

All the players begin searching the room for the button. If any player gets near the button, It says, "Warm!" If a player gets very close, It says, "Hot! Hot!" But which player is hot? If no player is anywhere near the button, It can say, "Cold! Freezing!" Whoever finds the button is the next It.

Homonyms

Type:	Word
Object:	Have fun thinking up homonyms
Players:	2 or more
Ages:	4 and older; able to understand the concept
Where:	On a car trip or anywhere
Equipment:	None

Homonyms are two (or more) words that sound exactly alike but have completely different meanings. They may be spelled alike, as in elephant's *trunk* and storage *trunk*, or vampire *bat* and baseball *bat*. Or they may be spelled differently: *bear, bare* or *see, sea*. (This point will not matter, of course, to prereaders!) To play, one player just announces, "Homonyms!" The players then think as hard as they can. The first person to come up with a homonym wins! No points, no score—the real object is for players to use their noggins. Players congratulate each other heartily for discovering special and unique homonyms. Older players also have fun announcing their homonyms in the form of a sentence, getting as fancy as they like.

Homonym Detective

Type: Word
Object: Come up with homonyms that are difficult to guess
Players: 2 or more
Ages: 9 and older
Where: On a car trip or anywhere
Equipment: None

It thinks up a pair of homonyms, then gives clues in the form of a sentence: "I can view the ocean." Answer? "I can *see* the *sea*." Or, "My fifty-two players are on the wooden patio." Answer? "My *deck* (of playing cards, which number fifty-two) is on the *deck*." Players may keep score by awarding a point to whomever thinks up a fair homonym that no other player is able to guess. The game is also great just for the fun of it. The first person to guess a homonym gets to be It, or players may just take turns.

86

Homonyms in the Teakettle

Type: Word
Object: Come up with homonyms that are difficult to guess
Players: 2 or more
Ages: 9 and older
Where: On a car trip or anywhere
Equipment: None

As with Homonym Detective, players give clues in sentences. But for Homonyms in the Teakettle, a player substitutes the word *teakettle* for each homonym in the sentence. The other players then must guess the words the player has in mind. For instance, a player might say, "Let's pick that teakettle of teakettles from the tree."

The answer is, "Let's pick that *pair* of *pears*!" Players may keep score (a point to whoever thinks up a homonym no one can guess) or just play for the fun of it. The first person to guess a homonym gets to be It, or players may take turns.

Hopscotch

Type:	Hop and target throw
Object:	Make it through the diagram the right way and first
Players:	2–4 (and slightly more in some games)
Ages:	6 and older
Where:	Outdoors, gym
Equipment:	Markers and chalk

In basic Hopscotch, the players draw a numbered diagram, usually in chalk on pavement. A very common Hopscotch diagram is shown here. Hopscotch patterns come in many forms, and Hopscotch games with many variations in rules. Some are given here, but players often get creative and draw patterns to suit themselves. For all Hopscotch games, two or more players take turns hopping through the segments in a particular way. They usually use markers to show their progress. (Players should choose distinctive markers—stones they can tell apart, different coins, whatever. Serious Hopscotch players have special lucky markers that are unique.)

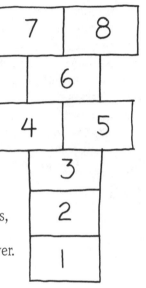

Different Hopscotch games have different rules about how the players hop. Usually, players must avoid squares that hold the markers of the other players, and sometimes they must avoid their own markers. Also, when thrown, a player's marker must land inside the right segment, or that player's turn is over.

Typical Rules and Variations
The following rules are typical of most Hopscotch games:

- Generally, when a player hops on one foot, she must keep hopping on the same foot until (and unless) she reaches the special segments that must be hopped on in special ways for certain games. Players must *hop*, not step, from segment to segment.
- In games where players hop to one end of a pattern and back, players may decide to face backward on the way back.
- Often for games where players hop to one end of a pattern and back, they must hop over their own markers on the way there but may land on their own markers on the way back.
- One turn may consist of one player's going to the end and back, if she can do it successfully. Then it's the next player's turn. Or a player may, during one turn, keep on playing, going there and back, there and back, moving her marker, until she makes an error. If the first player gets all the way through the game in her first turn, a tie is the best the others can do. But next time they can make the game more difficult!
- When a player tosses her marker, if she misses the square she's shooting for, her turn is over. Or, each player could have two tries to throw the marker where it should go.
- Usually, if a player lands in a square that she shouldn't have landed in (for instance, one that holds another player's marker), her turn is over.
- If a player's foot lands on a line, she loses her turn. Or, players may decide that as long as the foot is more in (where it should be) than out, that's OK.
- If a player makes an error, her turn is over. On her next turn, she resumes playing from where she was at the *beginning* of the turn where she messed up.

Classic Hopscotch

Note: No more than four players should play at once. Otherwise, the Hopscotch board will get too crowded with markers.

The first player throws her marker onto square 1, then jumps into 2 on one foot. She then hops on one foot to square 3, then to 4 and 5 at once, landing with one foot in each. Next, she lands with one foot in 6, then one foot in 7, one each in 8 and 9 at the same time, one in 10, and two feet in 11. Now she jumps up into the air, turns halfway around, reversing the position of her feet. She then hops back to square 1 the same way. Before jumping into square 1, she picks up her marker, then jumps into 1 and hops out of the diagram. (Players may not land in any square that holds a marker, not even their own.) After hopping out, she turns around and tosses her marker into square 2, where it will stay until her next turn.

Now it's the other player's turn. The next player puts his marker into 1, then starts by jumping all the way into 3, since he can't land on squares that hold his marker or hers.

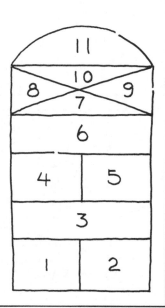

The players continue taking turns. Anytime a player makes an error—throws her marker and misses the right square, lands on the line, jumps in a square where there's a marker—her turn is over, and the player does not advance. The first player to get her marker to segment 11 wins. Players may also play to 11 *and* back if they like.

89

English Hopscotch

Note: Players need *big* markers—blocks, Koosh balls, or such.

The English Hopscotch diagram is quite distinct. The object is to move from square 1 to square 6, but . . .

4.	5.	6.
3.	2.	1.

. . . when a player hops, he holds his marker between his feet or legs. The player must take only one hop to go from space to space, and . . .

. . . he must not drop his marker, and . . .

. . . he must hop *entirely* into the next square. Hops must be taken in order (1 to 2, 2 to 3, and so on). Players may attempt to take another hop after making it safely into a square on one turn, but they must hop from where they landed without dropping the marker. If a player fails to hop clearly and cleanly into the next square, on his next turn he may move closer to the line to hop.

Tic Tac Hopscotch

Note: No markers are needed.

In Tic Tac Hopscotch, the first player hops through the squares in order. She must land on one foot only in each square, one at a time in order, including 1/2, 4/5, and 8/9 (no both-feet-down at the same time). When the player makes it all the way to 10 and back, she takes the chalk and writes her initial in any one space. The next player must hop over this space (not in it) to the next free number in order. On her next turn, when the first player comes to a square with her initial, she may stop and rest there with both feet. If she makes an error—lands on the line or out of the diagram, jumps into a space where someone else's initial is—her turn is over, and she doesn't get to put her initial down that time. Eventually, the diagram will become impassable. At this point, the player with the most initialed places wins.

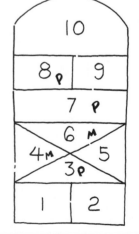

90

Horse

Type: Pickup basketball
Object: Copy the other player's shots
Players: 2
Ages: 7 and older
Where: A basketball court
Equipment: Basketball hoop and 1 ball for each player

Horse may be the most popular pickup basketball game for just two players. Players take turns shooting. The first player to go takes any kind of shot he chooses—overhand shot, jump shot, anything—from any spot on the court. If he makes his shot, . . .

. . . the next player must try the same shot from the same spot. If she successfully copies his shot, she may then design a shot for him to copy. But, if she fails to copy the shot, she gets the letter *H,* and her turn is over. Every time a player misses a shot someone else designed, she gets a new letter: *O, R, S,* and then *E.*

The lead passes back and forth as players try to make shots, with the task of designing shots . . .

. . . passing back and forth between the players. The first player to spell out HORSE loses.

Hot Potato

Type: Tossing
Object: Avoid getting stuck with the potato
Players: 4 or more
Ages: 6 and older
Where: Outdoors, gym, or other large indoor space
Equipment: Potato, beanbag, Nerf ball or such

The players sit in a circle, and It stands outside with his back turned to the others. The players in the circle begin tossing the potato to one another.

Once the potato is going, players may throw it around the circle in any direction, even across, as fast as they can.

Suddenly, It yells, "Hot!" The player holding the potato when It yells is out. If the potato is in the air, the last player to touch it is out. Keep throwing until only one player is left—the winner!

Huckleberry Finn

Type:	Searching
Object:	Find the object
Players:	5 or more
Ages:	5 and older
Where:	Usually indoors
Equipment:	Small object to hide

One player is It. All the other players leave the room, and It stays behind and hides the object. (A button, pencil, bottlecap, or other similar thing will do.) It doesn't hide the object completely, but leaves part of it showing.

The players return to the room and begin looking. It should be careful not to look at the hidden object! The first player to see the button says, "Huckleberry Finn," and sits down. One by one, the players see the button, say, "Huckleberry Finn," and sit.

The last player to spot the hidden object takes the letter *H*. (The second time that person is last, he takes *U*, then *C*, and then *K*.) Several rounds are played. The first player to spell HUCK loses. The first player who spots the object in each round gets to be It for the next round.

Hundred-Mile Race

Type: Board game
Object: Win the race
Players: 2–5
Ages: 5 and older (players on the young end of the range will need help creating the course)
Where: Indoors or out
Equipment: Material for course depending on how it's designed; playing pieces (small metal cars, plastic dinosaurs, shells, coins); one or more dice

First, players make their course: a long road divided into squares. They might draw it on pavement with chalk, use markers and cardboard, or count out boards of a wooden floor and mark them with removable tape. The main thing is to mark out a hundred miles (one hundred squares). Each player throws the die (or dice) once and moves that many miles. If a player lands on a space occupied by an opponent, he must immediately throw the die again and go that many spaces backward. The first to finish the race wins.

Variations:

- Four or more players can play in teams. To win, all members of one team must finish before another team does. It's OK for team members to land on each other's spot, and team members may give their turns to each other, even after throwing the die. This helps them land on an opponent's place and send him back.
- Players can run the race there *and* back and use two dice. If a player throws doubles, she takes twice the number of miles. If she throws dice that add up to seven, she gets to move and then roll the dice again.
- Players may use any other option they agree will make the game interesting!

I Doubt It

Type: Card
Object: Be first to use up cards
Players: 3–7
Ages: 7 and older
Where: Anywhere
Equipment: Deck of playing cards

The dealer deals seven cards to every player and lays the other cards facedown in a neat pile (the drawing pile). Then, from his own hand, the dealer lays a card (or cards) facedown on the table, announcing their value: "These are three sevens." (This starts the discard pile.) The next player (the one to the dealer's left) adds cards of the next highest value to the discard pile. Because the dealer said "three sevens," the next player must lay one or more eights facedown. If that player doesn't have any eights, she has a choice: she may discard one or more cards face down and *claim* they are eights. If she does this, the next player to the left may challenge by saying, "I doubt it." The player must then show the cards that were supposed to be eights. They're not eights, so she must take all the cards in the discard pile. If they had been eights, the challenger would be the one forced to take the discard pile.

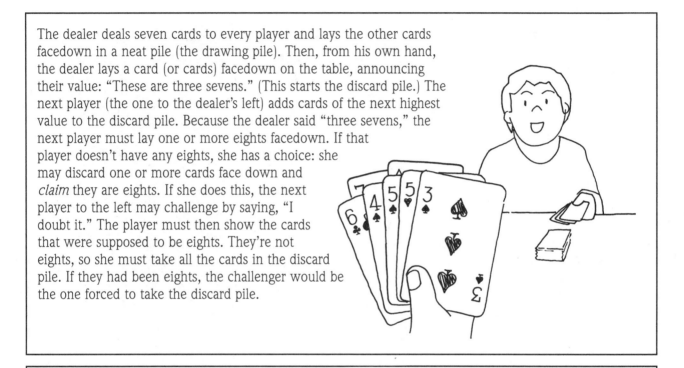

Or the player with no eights may draw a card from the drawing pile and make no discard. This is a safer choice, but a player can't get rid of cards this way! The players take turns around and around the table. The first player with no cards wins the hand. The first player to win three hands wins the game.

I Spy

Type: Guessing
Object: Guess something that starts with a certain letter
Players: 2 or more
Ages: 7 and older; able to spell well enough
Where: On a car trip or anywhere
Equipment: None

Two kids in a backseat can play this on a long trip, or a dozen can play indoors on a rainy day. For indoors, though, the more cluttered the area, the better! The first player to be It silently chooses an object everyone can see. It says, "I spy with my little eye something that begins with the letter *C*" (or whatever letter the object begins with). The other players take turns guessing, naming things that start with *C*.

Each time someone guesses wrong, It says, "No, it's not that." When someone gets it right, she's It. With just two players (It plus the guesser), the guesser gets no more than ten guesses. If she doesn't get it after ten, It gets to be It again. With more than two players, whoever guesses right first gets to be It, and the players' total tries (one player at a time) are unlimited.

Indian Ball

Type: Pickup softball
Object: Change places with the batter
Players: 3 or more
Ages: 8 and older
Where: Ball field or other open area
Equipment: Bat, softball, gloves (optional)

One player bats first; the others are the fielders. The batter stands at Home, and the other players arrange themselves thirty-five feet and more away (depending on how good they are). The batter pitches to himself by tossing the ball straight up and, when it comes down, trying to hit it into the field. Batters get unlimited tries to do this. If a fielder catches a fly ball, great! She's the new batter.

But if a fielder catches a grounder, the batter lays the bat down. The fielder with the ball rolls or throws from where she caught it.

If the fielder hits the bat, she gets to bat—*unless* the ball hits the bat, pops up, and the batter catches it before it comes back to the ground. If that happens, the batter remains at bat.

Jacks

Type: Ball toss and pickup
Object: Bounce the ball and pick up jacks in a prescribed way
Players: 2 or more
Ages: 6 and older
Where: Indoors or out
Equipment: Jacks and a small bouncy ball

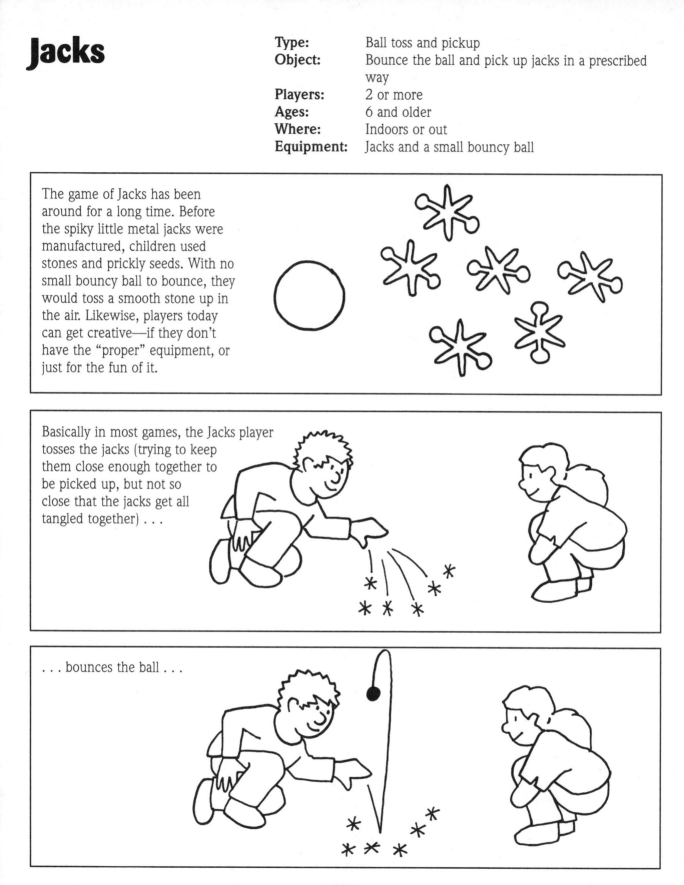

The game of Jacks has been around for a long time. Before the spiky little metal jacks were manufactured, children used stones and prickly seeds. With no small bouncy ball to bounce, they would toss a smooth stone up in the air. Likewise, players today can get creative—if they don't have the "proper" equipment, or just for the fun of it.

Basically in most games, the Jacks player tosses the jacks (trying to keep them close enough together to be picked up, but not so close that the jacks get all tangled together) . . .

. . . bounces the ball . . .

. . . then picks up some of the jacks in a particular way . . .

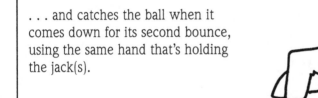

. . . and catches the ball when it comes down for its second bounce, using the same hand that's holding the jack(s).

The basics

There are some basic dos and don'ts of Jacks playing. And, of course, players may adapt these rules to suit themselves, so long as everyone agrees.

- A player may use only one hand to catch and pick up the jacks.
- A player may not touch the ball and jacks with her other hand, body, or clothes during a turn.
- The ball may bounce only once during a play.
- After a player tosses the jacks at the start of her turn, she must play them as they land.
- A player may take only one try at a particular play; if she makes an error, her turn is over.
- On a play, a player may touch only the jacks she's picking up. If she's on threesies, for instance, she may not touch or jar a fourth jack, or her turn is over.
- Players must take turns and keep playing in the same order.
- When a player makes an error, her turn is over. On her next turn, she must resume playing *at the beginning* of the turn where she made the mistake.

Left-handed players should note that for any instruction here that says to do something with the left or right hand, they should do the opposite!

Following are a few of the many popular Jacks games.

Eggs in the Basket
The player tosses six jacks, bounces the ball, . . .

. . . picks up one jack, puts it in her left hand ("the basket"), . . .

. . . and catches the ball. She counts "one," then continues bouncing and picking up the jacks, counting "two," "three," and so on for each jack picked up and transferred to her left hand. When she has picked up all six jacks, she scatters them again, then begins picking them up and counting—starting where she left off (seven, eight, and so on). The player continues until she makes a mistake, then her turn is over, and her score is the highest count she reached. The next player then does the same. High score wins.

Variation: Each player alternates taking two or more turns, and the final score is the total of all of a player's turns.

Onesies Twosies

Many Jacks games use the basic format of Onesies Twosies, with various twists and turns. In the basic game, the player tosses six jacks down. On her first throw (onesies), she bounces the ball, picks up one jack with her right hand, then catches the ball in the same hand. Then she puts the jack in her left hand and repeats the play until she has picked up all the jacks, one by one.

If she succeeds at onesies, she goes again, this time picking up *two* jacks at a time (twosies). For twosies, the player bounces, picks up two jacks, catches, then repeats until all jacks have been safely transferred to the other hand. Then she goes on, doing the same for threesies.

2

2 + 2

2 + 2 + 2

For foursies and fivesies, the player first picks up the large number (four or five), then on the second bounce, the one or two jacks left over. For sixies, the player picks up all the jacks at once. The first player to make it all the way through sixies wins.

Players should remember who went first, because a tie is possible. If two players make it through sixies at the end of their third turns, to break the tie they play back to fivesies, foursies, and so on. Whoever gets the furthest in one turn wins. Also, throughout play, anytime a player makes a mistake, her turn is over. On her next turn she must go back to the beginning of the turn (onesies, threesies, whatever) where she made the mistake.

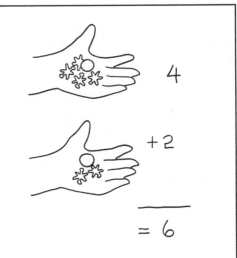

4

+2

_____

= 6

Pigs in the Pen

With her left hand, the player creates a "pigpen," where she'll transfer the jacks. With her right hand, she scatters six or more jacks, tosses the ball, slides or flicks one jack into the pen, and catches the ball. She may roll her hand up on its side to welcome the jack, then close it over the jack, but she may not move her left hand or use it to capture jacks. The players play onesies, twosies, on up to sixies or more. If a player fails to get the right number of jacks in the pen on a try, her turn is over.

Scrubs

The player slides the jacks (six or more) quickly back and forth across the playing surface with her right hand (called *scrubbing*), then scatters them, tosses the ball, picks up one jack, scrubs that jack, and catches the ball.

She must hold the picked-up jack in her right hand as she catches the ball with that hand. She may then transfer the jack(s) to her left hand, and go again—toss, pickup, scrub, and catch—until she makes a mistake. Each player goes from onesies through sixies (or more), so long as she gets the right number of jacks on every try and remembers to scrub at the right time.

Sheep over the Fence

The player puts her left hand and forearm on the playing surface to make a "fence." She scatters six or more jacks on one side of the fence. She tosses the ball, picks up one jack, . . .

. . . places the jack over the fence, . . .

. . . and catches the ball. Players should not *throw* the jacks over the fence, but *place* them. The play continues from onesies through twosies to sixies or more. The player must get the right number of jacks over the fence, or her turn is over.

Jambalaya Relay

Type:	Relay race
Object:	Complete the race first
Players:	6 or more in 2 or more teams
Ages:	6 and older
Where:	Outdoors, gym
Equipment:	Something to use as a baton (a stick, a plastic tube, even an inflated balloon on a string)

Jambalaya is a stew of many ingredients. In the game world, it's a spicy way to run a circle relay race. The players divide into teams and mark a racecourse. The length of the course depends on the age of the players and how the laps are to be run. (More on this later.) The course begins at a start line, goes a certain distance to a marked point, and circles back to the same line. Team members line up single file behind the start line. The first team members must run to the marked point and back, holding their team's baton. Anyone who drops a baton must stop and pick it up before continuing. When the runners return to the finish line, they relay the baton to their team's next racer, who then goes.

But in Jambalaya Relay, not all racers *run*. Whenever the baton changes hands, the new racers must get to the marker and back some other way. For instance, all the second racers crawl, the third ones run backward, the fourths skip, the fifths hop, and so on. (The players design the laps to suit themselves before the race starts.) The team that gets all its runners there and back first wins. Teams can strategize by giving the straight run to their faster member, the crawl to the most sturdily dressed, and so on. If a player forgets and races in the wrong manner, that player's team loses!

Jingle Tag

Type: Tag with blindfold
Object: Tag It
Players: 4 or more
Ages: 5 and older
Where: Outdoors, gym
Equipment: Lots of blindfolds; a jingle bell, tambourine, or other noisemaker; chalk

In this reverse Blindman's Buff, the players draw a circle or mark off the corner of a gym. All the players blindfold each other, except It. To start, It arranges the players along the borders of the play area, keeping the noisemaker quiet. Then It takes up a position and jingles the noisemaker. At this point, the players start looking for It, trying to tag her. Anytime It moves, she must sound the noisemaker. It must stay within the boundaries, so the players should make the area small enough that catching It is possible, but not too easy. Whoever catches It gets to be It the next time.

Keep-Away

Type:	Ball toss
Object:	Keep the ball away from the opponents
Players:	6 or more
Ages:	8 and older
Where:	Outdoors, gym
Equipment:	A rubber playground ball, a watch

Players divide into teams. They may set boundaries for play or may just play in a large area and go where the play takes them. To start, one team begins passing the ball back and forth, keeping it away from the opponents by throwing it over or around them. (A player who has the ball *may not* run while holding it. A player may take two steps while holding the ball, but no more.) The team with the ball counts each good pass it makes: one, two, three, and so on. The members of the other team continually try to capture the ball. When they do, they begin counting good passes. After ten minutes, the team that reached the highest number during a single count wins.

Variation: With only 3 players, two toss the ball to keep it away from the third. When the third intercepts the ball, she switches roles with the player who last threw the ball.

Kick the Can

Type:	Hiding and seeking
Object:	Come out of hiding and get home without being tagged
Players:	3 or more
Ages:	5 and older
Where:	Outdoors
Equipment:	An empty can

The players gather around their empty can.

One player (It) gives the can a good hard kick in any direction. All the other players run! It, meanwhile, runs after the can, . . .

. . . returns it to its original spot, closes his eyes, and counts to one hundred. It then shouts, "Ready or not, here I come!" He opens his eyes . . .

... and starts searching for the players. When It sees a player, he calls out the player's name, and the two race for the can.

If the player gets there first, the player is home free. But if It either reaches the can first or tags the player before they get there, the player is caught. The first caught player must be It next time, unless freed.

A caught player must stand at the can but can be freed if another hider reaches him without being tagged. The player kicks the can and yells, "Home free!" She and the already caught one are safe. It must set the can back up and keep searching. He must find all the players and keep at least one of them caught, or he'll have to be It again.

Killer Whale

Type: Tag
Object: Avoid getting caught by the Killer Whale
Players: 3 or more
Ages: 5 (in very shallow water with close supervision) and older
Where: In a pool
Equipment: None

Choose a player to be the Whale. The players get in the pool and mill about in the shallow or deep end, depending on swimming ability. The Whale gets right in the center of the playing area. Everyone knows who the Whale is and is careful not to get too close. But players *must* stay closer to the Whale than to the sides. The Whale starts out as a gentle black whale and paddles about with everyone else, acting innocent. But suddenly he shouts, "Killer whale!" . . .

. . . and tries to tag someone. The Whale may not tag or chase anyone until he has shouted, "Killer whale," and no one may head for the side until then either! Players who make it to the sides without getting tagged are safe. If any player gets tagged by the Whale, the round is over, and that player is the new Whale. If the Whale catches no one (everyone makes it to the sides), the Whale says, "Black whale," and everyone moves back toward the center until the killer comes out again.

Variation: Play Moby Dick.

King of the Hill

Type: Rough and tumble
Object: Be on top of the hill
Players: 3 or more
Ages: 6 and older
Where: Outdoors on a hill, mound, or pile of gravel
Equipment: None

Players find a nice hill to play on, then choose a player to be King first.

The King braces himself on top of the hill, and the other players rush him, trying to push him from the hill. Players may use hands, backs, or shoulders to push, but pushing only! No hair pulling, kicking, or other brutality.

Players can dethrone Kings at any time, but strength is not all that matters. Sometimes while two stronger players struggle, . . .

. . . a weaker one takes the hill!

Variations: Large groups may vary the game as follows:

- The group may choose a referee. The ref keeps score by giving a point to a player every time she takes the top, even if only for a second. Whoever is ahead after five minutes wins.
- Or the group can play in teams, with teammates defending one of their own who makes it to the top.

Lean-Two

Type:	Group coordination
Object:	Giggles galore as players move back and forth in a circle and try not to bump heads
Players:	6 or more (in even numbers)
Ages:	5 and older
Where:	Outdoors, gym
Equipment:	None

The group of players stands in a circle holding hands. Every other player is a One; each of the others is a Two. One of the players is also the Caller.

When the Caller says, "One!" all the Ones lean in, and all the Twos lean out. As soon as everyone is all balanced, the Caller yells, "Two!" The Twos go in, and the Ones go out. Continuing in this way, It picks up the pace until the circle is vibrating like a rubber band.

They keep going till everyone falls down laughing.

Leapfrog

Type: Jumping relay race
Object: Make it to the finish line first
Players: 6 or more
Ages: 5 and older
Where: Outdoors, gym
Equipment: None

The players divide into teams of two and mark start and finish lines. The length of the race will depend on the age of the players. To begin, one member of each team crouches at the start line. From a few feet behind the start line, the other partner takes a running start . . .

. . . and hops over her crouching teammate. A good technique is for a player to put her hands on her partner's shoulders and push herself up and over her partner's head.

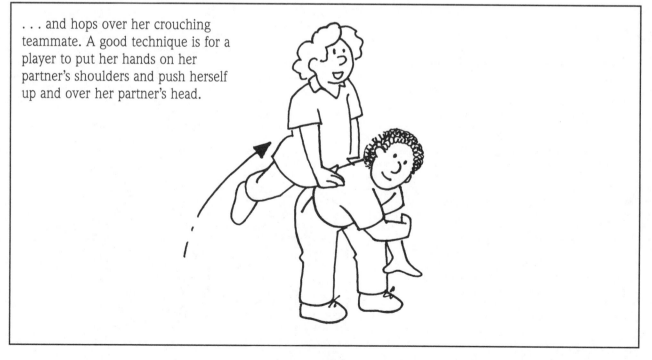

She lands and crouches down in front of her partner.

Now he takes his turn: he goes back to the start line, runs forward, and leaps over her. They take turns until they both cross the finish line. The first team to cross the finish line wins.

Players may also play three on a team. The first leaper stays down in front of the croucher, and the third team member then leaps over them both, one at a time. So they go, all the way to the finish line.

Variation: For younger players, the pair could simply crouch and leap over each other again and again without running back to start each time.

London Bridge

Type: Sing-song and tug-of-war
Object: (Accidentally) get on the strongest team for the tug-of-war
Players: 5 or more
Ages: 6 and older
Where: Outdoors, gym, or large open room
Equipment: None

Two players are chosen to make a bridge. But before they form the bridge, they put their heads together and secretly decide which of them will be Silver, which Gold. Then they clasp hands and raise their arms in an arch (the bridge). The other players circle under the bridge singing:

London Bridge is falling down,

Falling down, falling down.

London Bridge is falling down,

My fair lady.

When they sing, "My fair lady," the bridge drops. (The partners lower their arms, with hands still clasped.) Whoever is caught inside the arms is a Prisoner. The Prisoner must whisper to the bridge players either "silver" or "gold." The bridge players then stand the Prisoner behind the one of them he (unknowingly) chose. The singing and circling begins again and continues until all the players are prisoners and lined up behind a bridge player.

At this point, the gold and silver teams face off for a tug-of-war. Gold and Silver clasp hands, and the gold and silver Prisoners line up behind them, holding each other by the waist. The first team that topples forward loses. If almost everybody chose either gold or silver, this contest won't last long!

Marbles

Type: Target shooting with marbles
Object: Hit the target as required in a particular game
Players: 5 or more
Ages: 6 and older
Where: Outdoors, gym, or large open room
Equipment: Marbles

Marbles come in many sizes, shapes, and types. They are not only playing equipment, they're collector's items and the prize that players get for winning. But players should be warned: the game of Marbles is often played for keeps. When players lose their marbles in a game, they *really* lose them. If players don't want to play for keeps, they can play for score. But usually the chance of winning or losing marbles is what makes the game exciting. *Before they start*, players should be clear whether they are playing for keeps!

Marbles can be played on smooth dirt, asphalt, tile, wood, or carpet. To mark the playing area, players can scratch lines into dirt or use chalk to mark harder surfaces. The playing surface will have a definite effect on the behavior of the marbles. Hard, smooth, level surfaces help marbles go fast and straight. Players should remember, too, when drawing circles and lines, to match the distances to the skill and number of players and to the playing surface.

How to Shoot

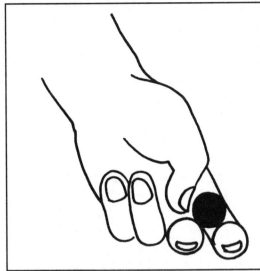

Marbles players bowl or shoot one marble to hit and win marbles from other players. Some games, especially dropping and tossing games, define how the players must shoot. But generally, when a player is down on the ground shooting a marble across the surface, the most accurate shooting method is to hold the marble between forefinger and middle finger, lightly pressing the forefinger knuckle to the ground. From this position, the player thumb-flicks the marble out of his hand toward the target.

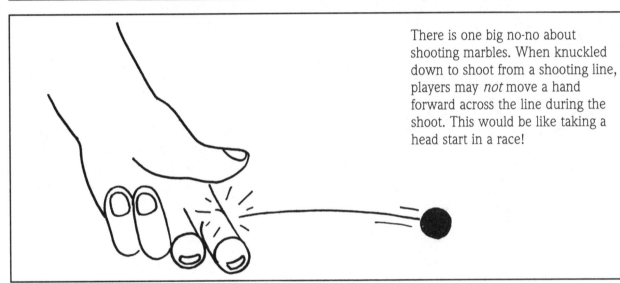

There is one big no-no about shooting marbles. When knuckled down to shoot from a shooting line, players may *not* move a hand forward across the line during the shoot. This would be like taking a head start in a race!

Who Shoots First?

The Introduction gives some ways to choose which player will go first. Players can use one of these to decide who shoots first, but there's also a special way, called *lagging*, to choose who gets to start off in Marbles. To lag, players draw a target line. Everyone steps back and shoots from the same spot. To win the lag, a player's marble must stop the closest to the target line without going over it. The player who comes next closest goes second, and so on. In games where going last is better (like Spangie) the closest marble goes last, the next closest next to last, and so on.

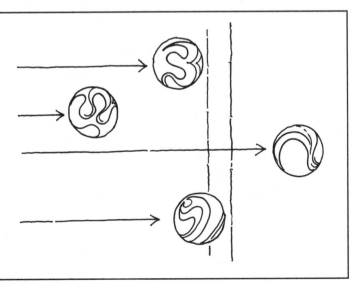

Many Different Ways to Play

There are many kinds of Marbles. The games described here are just samples, and players should feel free to change and adapt these games to suit themselves. Players should just make sure everyone understands and agrees to the rules before starting. For instance, kids often shoot with special marbles, called *taws*, that are a little bigger than the target marbles. Players should decide whether this is a rule or an option. Or, when it comes to "hitting" marbles to win, players should decide before starting whether a player must actually hit the marble or just get within a certain distance—say, the span between the player's thumb and forefinger.

Bossout

The first player shoots a marble any distance. From the same spot, another player shoots at the first marble; if he hits it, he takes it. But if he misses, he leaves his marble down, and the next shooter aims for it. Each new shooter puts a new marble into play. With only two players, they simply alternate turns, still adding a marble each time. The first player who strikes (or comes close enough to) the last marble shot wins *all* the marbles.

Chasies

Chasies can be played any old place (a smooth surface, grass, gravel, anywhere in the yard), and lots of players can play. Players decide on the order of play before starting and stick to it. The first player drops a marble, and everyone takes ten steps away from it. Now everyone takes a turn throwing underhanded to hit the dropped marble. When a player hits the first target marble, he takes that marble, and the next player in turn must put down one of her marbles as the target before shooting. All the shooting marbles stay down until everyone has had a turn.

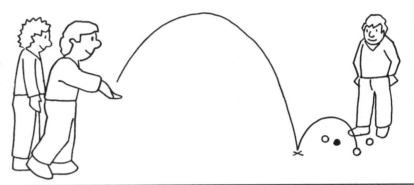

If everyone takes a turn and no one hits the original target, the player who got closest gets to try a drop shot. He picks up his marble, holds it out over the target marble from shoulder level, and drops it. If he hits the target marble, he gets it. If he misses, the player who dropped the original target marble picks it up, and the second player puts down a new target marble for the next round.

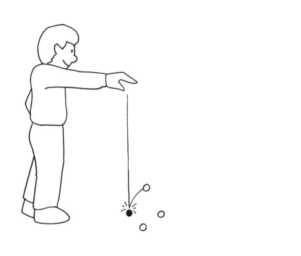

Hundreds

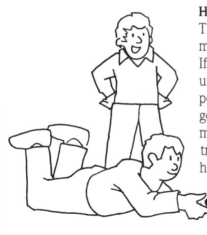

The game of Hundreds is played on dirt by two players. The players make a small hole in the ground, then take turns shooting a marble at it. If both players get a marble in the hole, no one scores. They try again until only one of them lands a marble in the hole. That's worth 10 points. They keep shooting until someone makes 100 points. That player gets to try for the championship. First, he shoots once at the hole. If he makes it, the game is over, and he wins. If he misses, the other player tries. That player gets 10 points for getting in the hole. However, if he hits the first marble instead, he gets an instant 100 points and may also try for the championship. Whoever shoots straight into the hole first wins. If the players both get in on the first try, they keep taking shots until someone misses.

Obstacle Course

In Obstacle Course, the players *do* want to hit the obstacles. First, they arrange four or more objects, ranging in size from a baseball to a bucket, and name what the shooting order of the objects will be. Fixed objects such as clothesline poles or table legs are OK. Starting at the same spot, the players take turns shooting a marble at the obstacles in order, trying to hit each obstacle. A player who hits the object does not move his or her marble, but shoots it from where it landed at the next object. Players keep shooting until they miss, then they leave the marble where it landed and the next player goes. The first shooter to hit the last obstacle does not automatically win. Instead, the player must shoot his marble from where it landed and hit another player's marble. If he hits one, the marble's owner is out of the game. Play then continues, turn by turn. When it's the turn of the player who finished the course, he may try again to hit another player. But he may choose not to, because if he misses, he is eliminated. Usually, players will lie in wait and only shoot for marbles they are sure to hit. Play continues until only one player is left. That player is the winner and gets all the marbles.

Poison Ring

This is a kind of backward Ringer. Many can play, and the circle can be made smaller than the ten feet across recommended for Ringer, if the players choose. Each player puts in the same number of marbles: three or four. They clump all the marbles in the center of the circle. A player sets up anywhere outside the circle and shoots. She tries to knock a target marble out and have her shooter go out.

Only if her shooter goes out does she get to keep any target marbles she shoots out. After her shot, the other players take their turns. Each shooter gets *one* shot per turn. Whoever has the most marbles at the end wins. Players may decide that the winner then wins all the marbles that everyone else took, or that the players all keep the marbles they shot out.

121

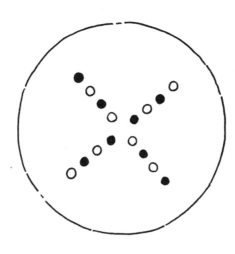

Potsies

The players draw a big circle, at least seven feet across. They all put in an equal number of marbles and form the marbles into an X in the center of the circle.

A player's goal is to knock a marble out of the circle but keep her shooter marble *inside* the circle. Every time a player succeeds, she may shoot again. As soon as she misses, her turn is over. If she knocks out a marble *and* her shooter, her turn is over, and she must return the target marble to the circle. As soon as one player wins more marbles than she put in at the beginning, that player wins big. She wins *all* the marbles put in at the beginning, even those taken by other players during the round.

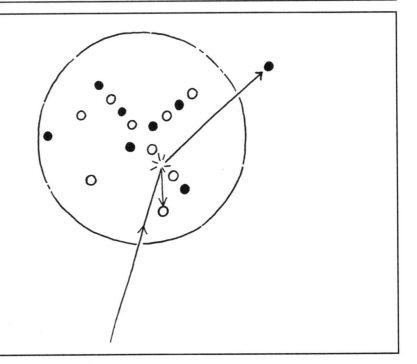

Ring and Line

The players draw a circle and, at a distance outside the circle, a shooting line. Each player puts the same number of marbles in the circle, clumped in the middle or however else suits them. All players take turns shooting from the line into the circle of marbles. The object is to knock the marbles out of the circle. A player keeps any marbles she knocks out, but only if her shooter goes out.

If her shooter stays in, she loses it. Her "lost" marble becomes one of the target marbles, and she must shoot with a fresh one next time.

A player doesn't get the target marble just for hitting it. She must hit it *out*.

If a player misses the ring altogether, or shoots straight through it without hitting a marble, she keeps her marble, but her turn is over.

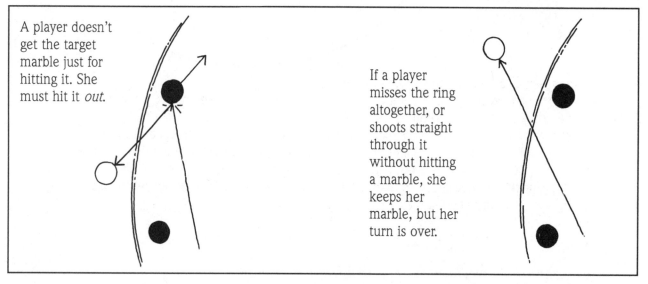

123

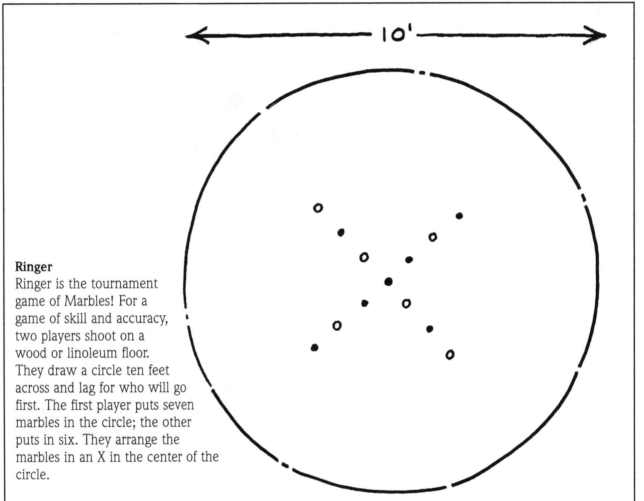

Ringer

Ringer is the tournament game of Marbles! For a game of skill and accuracy, two players shoot on a wood or linoleum floor. They draw a circle ten feet across and lag for who will go first. The first player puts seven marbles in the circle; the other puts in six. They arrange the marbles in an X in the center of the circle.

Players *must* keep one knuckle down while shooting.

The player's goal is to knock a marble out of the circle and, if possible, keep his shooting marble *in* the circle. Players take turns shooting. On a turn, if a player shoots one or more marbles out of the circle, he keeps those marbles and shoots again from where his shooter stopped. If he shoots one or more marbles out of the circle and his shooter goes out, he keeps the target marbles, but his turn is over. If he shoots and hits no marbles out of the circle, his turn is over. He picks up his shooter. On his next turn, he shoots from anywhere outside the circle. The first player to take seven marbles wins all thirteen marbles.

Spangie

Spangie is played at a wall or the foundation of a house. The players establish a shooting line, then one player shoots a marble at the wall. The next player then shoots at the wall, trying to hit the first marble. The players continue taking turns, with the number of marbles on the ground steadily increasing, until someone makes the shot.

The first player to shoot, hit the wall, then strike any marble with her shooter takes *all* the marbles.

Variation: To make the game harder, players may specify that they can win only by shooting and hitting the last marble that was shot against the wall.

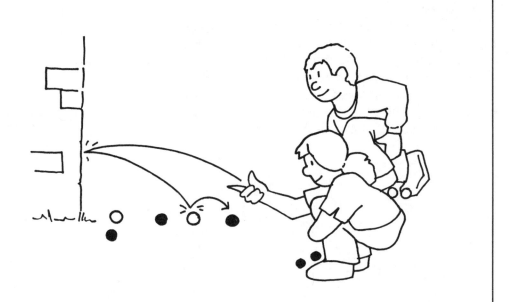

Straight Shot
Each player puts the same
number of marbles on a line. The
players then take turns shooting
at the line from the same spot.
Players keep any marbles they
knock off the line.

If a player misses
and hits no
marbles, she must
add another of her
marbles to the
line. The game
continues until all
the marbles have
been knocked off
the line.

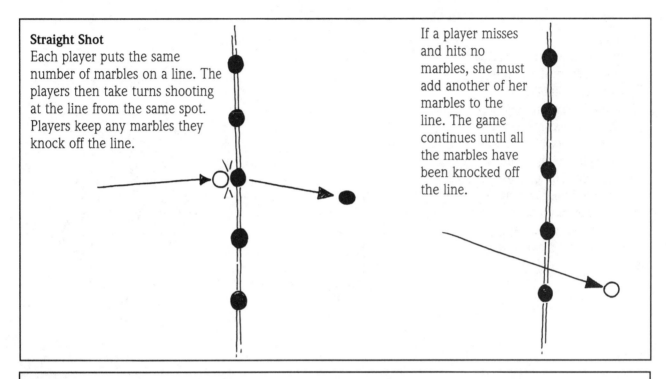

Tic Tac Taw
In Tic Tac Taw, a great two-player game of Marbles, the
players can decide whether to play with *taws* (special
shooting marbles) or regular marbles. Players draw a Tic-Tac-
Toe-like grid in the dirt or with chalk on pavement. Then
they move back a few steps and draw a shooting line.
Players then take turns, one shot per turn, trying to place
their own marbles within one of the places on the grid.

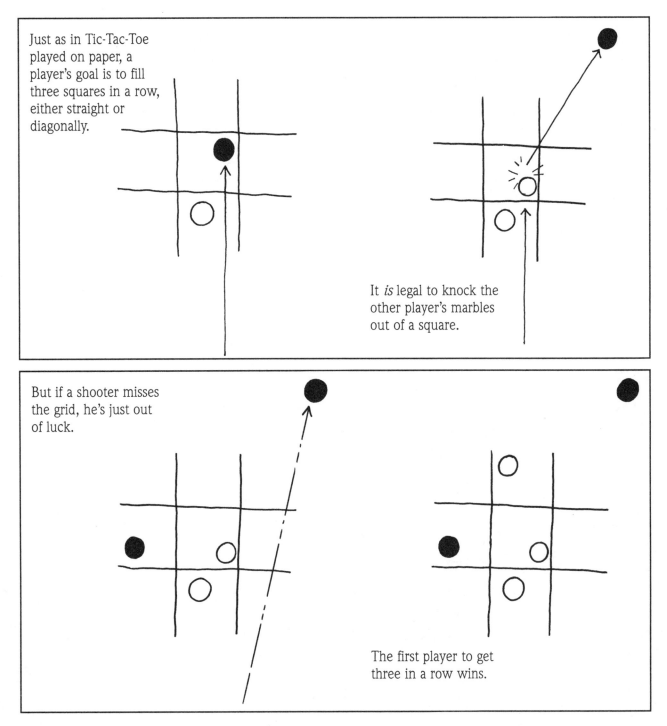

Just as in Tic-Tac-Toe played on paper, a player's goal is to fill three squares in a row, either straight or diagonally.

It *is* legal to knock the other player's marbles out of a square.

But if a shooter misses the grid, he's just out of luck.

The first player to get three in a row wins.

127

Marco Polo

Type: Tag
Object: Avoid getting tagged by It
Players: 4 or more
Ages: 7 and older
Where: In a pool
Equipment: Blindfold, if desired

One player is It. All the other players get in the pool and gather around It, who is "blind" for the round. (Usually, It simply keeps her eyes closed tightly, on her honor. An actual blindfold is OK, *with adult supervision*. Players can use blacked-out goggles or any kind of blindfold that will work *safely* in the water.) The game starts, and It must chase and tag another player. But how can a blind player possibly find and tag someone else? When It says, "Marco," . . .

. . . the other players *must* answer, "Polo!"

She locates a player with her ears and
goes after him.

The player who is tagged becomes It.

Memory

Type: Test of memory
Object: Remember where the card pairs are
Players: 2 or more
Ages: 5 and older
Where: On any flat surface
Equipment: Deck of playing cards

Take a regular deck of cards, shuffle them well, and lay all or part of them out facedown in neat rows. (If you use only a partial deck, make sure it consists entirely of matched pairs.) The first player turns two cards faceup so everyone can see them. If they match— unlikely at the start—the player takes the cards and tries again. (A match is two threes, tens, jacks, and so on, regardless of color.) If the two cards do not match, the player turns them back facedown, and the next player turns over two cards, looking for a pair.

As the game continues, and more and more cards are seen, there are fewer cards. Therefore, remembering where the cards are and finding pairs becomes easier. Every time a player finds a pair, she gets another turn. The player who takes the most pairs wins.

Variations: The game can be varied to make it harder or easier:

- For increased difficulty, use a whole deck and have only same-color pairs count as matches.
- To make an easier game for preschoolers, use only two suits, or leave out the face cards and aces.

Milk Caps (also known as POGS)

Type:	Unique tossing game
Object:	Get the milk caps to land in a certain way, to win caps or points
Players:	2 or more
Ages:	5 and older
Where:	On any hard, flat surface that can't be dented or damaged by the slammers
Equipment:	Caps and slammers

In the 1930s, a popular game was played with the cardboard caps of glass milk bottles. Players collected the caps and used them to play a game that consisted of stacking the caps and trying to knock them over in various ways. Sound familiar? Milk may not be delivered in glass bottles anymore, but kids are playing the game again. In the early 1990s, kids in Hawaii rediscovered Milk Caps, this time playing it with the tops of plastic juice bottles. In just a few years, the game of Milk Caps moved from Hawaii to California and all across the United States.

Today lots of kids collect the wildly decorated cardboard disks (caps) that are specially manufactured to play this game. Kids also collect the metal and plastic slammers they use to *slam*, or throw at the stacked caps. Collecting is one reason the game is so popular. In fact, building up a collection of caps is a central part of the game.

Usually, when players win caps in one game or another, they win them for keeps; the caps belong to them. When slamming for keeps, players should make sure everyone understands what this means before they start playing! Players may also play just for fun, returning all caps to their original owners at the end of play. Or players might compete for score, giving 1 point for each cap flipped. Players could play several different games of caps, then add all the scores for a grand total.

The game itself is fun, simple, and fast moving. There are just a few rules and a few optional ways to play the many, many games that kids have come up with. Players should agree on the rules and options before they start.

Basic Caps

Each player adds an equal number of caps to the stack, which is arranged picture side down. Players may include their caps in a chunk together or alternate them.

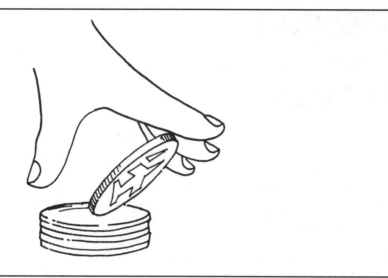

Players take turns hitting the stack of caps with a slammer. The player keeps any cap that lands with the picture up.

After a player slams and takes his winnings, he restacks the remaining caps for the next player.

Rules and Options

Letting go of the slammer. Almost always, when a player throws a slammer, he must release it *before* it touches the caps.

Misses. If a player slams and misses the stack of caps altogether, he gets to try again.

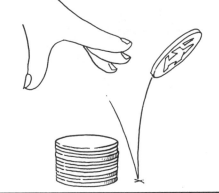

Pinch hitters. Players may ask a friend (or anyone who's a better slammer) to do the slam for them. They may offer this "pinch hitter" some of the winnings to do it, too.

Safety. If the stack of caps gets so short that players think they can't possibly flip any over, players may add some of their own caps, which they get back after the slam.

An option is whether to allow slaps. This means a player slaps a hand—the one not throwing the slammer—on the playing surface the instant the slammer comes down. Slaps can help to cause more flip-overs.

Players may also agree to allow tippies. A player using tippies presses a slammer down on the edge of the last cap left, trying to pinch the edge in such a way that the cap flips over.

Bomb

Bomb is for two players. One player places one cap faceup, then stacks another cap facedown on top of the first. The other player then adds two facedown caps to the stack.

4.

3.

2.

1.

The players take turns slamming.

Whoever gets all four caps to land faceup after a slam wins them all (or gets the points).

Freeze!

Each player uses an equal number of her own caps—at least five. All caps are stacked facedown. Right in the middle of the stack goes one slammer, also facedown.

There's a special rule about slamming in this game. A player must rest her slammer on the pads of her first and second fingers, then flip it over for the slam. The player must not pinch the slammer, grasp it in any way, or use her thumb.

The object is to slam and flip all the caps faceup at once. If a player does that, she yells, "Freeze!" She gets a point for every cap and 5 points for the slammer. She then restacks and lets the next player have a try. If the next player fails, the first yells, "Defreeze!" She gets the points again.

Players play as many turns as they want. The one with the highest score wins and, if playing for keeps, gets all the caps.

Magic

Each player stacks an equal number of his own caps—at least three—facedown. Right in the middle of the stack goes one faceup cap. The first player uses his slammer to just tap the top of the stack, then immediately yells, "Magic!" and slams. A player must do something quite difficult to win at Magic: split the stack into two facedown stacks, with the middle cap turned facedown. Players take turns trying until one player succeeds—and takes all.

Poison

Each player places an equal number of caps facedown in the stack. Players take turns slamming. The goal is to hit the stack and knock it down without flipping any caps faceup. If a player does this, she circles the caps with her slammer and says, "Poison." Players score a point per facedown cap, or—if all the caps are facedown and if playing for keeps—they get the entire stack.

Terminator

Each player uses an equal number of caps and stacks them facedown in one stack. Traditionally, players use metal slammers for this game, but they must use extra caution with play (and with the playing surface). The players take turns slamming, with the object of turning all the caps faceup in one slam.

The player who succeeds is the one and only winner.

Threesies

Each player adds three caps, facedown, to the stack.

The players take turns slamming, with the goal of flipping over at least three at once. If a player flips over fewer than three, the player gets nothing. If a player gets three or more, the player may go again. Play continues as long as enough caps remain in the stack.

Twosies

Twosies is for two players. Each player puts down only one cap—a very short stack indeed.

The players take turns slamming. The goal is to slam both caps faceup. Whoever does this keeps the caps. For the next round, the loser must contribute both caps. A game consists of six rounds.

Minicroquet

Type:	Ball rolling
Object:	Get a small ball in the target hole
Players:	2 or more
Ages:	6 and older
Where:	Outdoors
Equipment:	Golf or croquet balls

Players dig three shallow holes in a line. The holes should be just a bit larger than the balls and at least ten feet apart. The players also draw a serving line perpendicular to the row of holes. (The serving line and row of holes form a T.) Players take turns rolling for the holes.

A player starts with a heel on the serving line. He rolls his ball toward the first hole. If the ball lands in the hole, he takes the ball out, puts his heel near the hole, and rolls for the second hole. If the player makes it again, he puts his heel near *that* hole and rolls for the third one.

If the player misses at any time, his turn is over. His ball stays where it landed. He will start shooting from that spot, toward the hole he missed, on his next turn. The next player goes.

The next players may shoot for the holes just as the first did, or . . .

. . . they may shoot for a ball on the course. If a player strikes someone else's ball, he may roll his ball again from where it landed. But if a player rolls for and misses the other ball and/or the hole, his turn is over, and his ball stays where it landed. The winner is the first player to roll into the third hole, then back to the second and first, and again to the second and third.

Mnemonics

Type: Word
Object: Have the best memory
Players: 3 or more
Ages: 8 and older
Where: On a car trip or anywhere
Equipment: Paper and pencil

Mnemonics are everywhere. Television ads, for instance, use the numerical-alphabetical keypad on the telephone to make advertisers' phone numbers more memorable: "This car deal won't last! Telephone 1-800-NEW AUTO!"

Players can use the same keypad to play Mnemonics. (Let 1 be Z and 0 be Q.) Players write down their own and everyone else's seven-digit phone number. Let's say Deborah's number is 349-8369. Using the corresponding phone pad letters as illustrated here, each player creates a sentence to help remember Deborah's number. The first letter of each word in the sentence must correspond to the appropriate number on the keypad, to spell out her phone number. For example:

3 DEF **F**inally

4 GHI **I**

9 WXY **W**ill

8 TUV **U**nderstand

3 DEF **D**eborah's

6 MNO **O**dd

9 WXY **W**ays

Deborah collects the sentences, reads them out loud, and everyone votes for best sentence. Players may not vote for their own sentences. Everyone memorizes the mnemonic sentence that is voted best, then moves on to the next number. When each phone number has been played, the players put aside their lists and get out fresh paper. Go! The winner is the first player to write down every phone *number* correctly.

Moby Dick

Type: Water tag
Object: Get away from Moby Dick
Players: 5 or more
Ages: 5 (in very shallow water with close supervision) and older
Where: In a pool
Equipment: Pennies (1 for each player); a cup

Players choose a Whale by drawing lots. Everyone picks a penny from a cup. The one who picks a particular penny (the 1974 one, for instance) is the Whale. Without the Whale revealing his identity, the players all jump into the pool. Everyone mills about. They must stay closer to the center than to the sides. No one wants to get too close to anyone else, since the Whale could be anyone. But a player may not go for the side unless the Whale is chasing her! Without being obvious about it, the mystery Whale moves within striking distance.

Finally, the Whale yells, "Moby Dick!" and goes after someone, trying to tag that player.

Any players who reach the side without being tagged are safe. But if the Whale touches a player before the player can reach the side, that player is out of the game. If the Whale tags no one, the Whale is out of the game. The remaining players draw pennies again for a new secret Whale and play another round. The last player to survive wins.

Variation: Play Killer Whale.

Monkey in the Middle

Type: Ball keep-away
Object: Keep the ball away from the player in the middle
Players: 3
Ages: 6 and older
Where: Outdoors, gym
Equipment: Rubber playground ball

Two of the players stand twelve to fifteen feet apart, with the third player (the Monkey) between them. The two throwers toss the ball back and forth, trying not to let the player in the middle grab or deflect the ball.

If the Monkey gets the ball, . . .

. . . the last player who touched it must be the new Monkey in the middle. Every time a player becomes a Monkey, the player gets a point. (The first player to be the Monkey doesn't get a point for that.) Play continues until one player has 11 points. Then the player with the fewest points wins.

Mother, May I?

Type: Follow Mother's instructions
Object: Reach Mother first
Players: 3 or more
Ages: 5 and older
Where: Outdoors, gym, or other large enough indoor space
Equipment: None

The players mark start and finish lines. One player is the Mother, and she stands alone at the finish line. All the other players line up at the start line for the "race." Mother starts the game by instructing the first player how he may move closer to Mother: "Tom, you may take one baby step." Tom replies, "Mother, may I?" Mother says, "You may." Then Tom takes his baby step. But if Tom forgets to ask, "Mother, may I?" not only may he *not* take his step, he must go back to the beginning.

Here are just a few of the steps Mother might give:

A *baby step* is one foot-length forward.

A *giant step* is a stride in which the player stretches as far as possible.

A *hop* involves hopping one step on one foot.

A *bunny hop* means a hop with both feet together.

141

A *scissors jump* is a one-foot-forward leap.

Hop and back means two hops forward, then one back.

Run means to run until told to stop, which will be almost immediately.

A *backward step* may be toward or away from Mother—whichever she specifies.

Blind means a regular step taken with closed eyes.

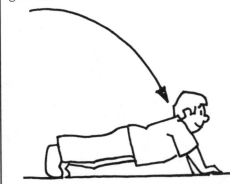

Caterpillar involves stepping to the farthest place the player can reach while his hands are on the ground.

Mother may also combine steps (one baby step plus one scissors jump, for instance) or invent steps as she goes along.

Players may move only as Mother says but try to cover as much distance as they can. Also, after properly asking, "Mother, may I?" a player may be told, "No, you may not." Mother may give second and third instructions before granting permission. She's trying to confuse the player into making an error!

Players must go back to the start line if they make an error (forgetting to ask, "Mother, may I?" or failing to follow instructions). The first player to reach the finish line is the winner.

Mousetrap

Type:	Running and catching
Object:	Avoid getting caught
Players:	7 or more
Ages:	6 and older
Where:	Outdoors, gym, or other large enough indoor space
Equipment:	None

One player is the Cat, one the Mouse. The other players hold hands in a circle. The players keep their arms raised to let the Mouse in and out. In the meantime, the Cat faces away; he's "asleep." The Mouse runs in and out and is safe as long as the Cat is sleeping.

Suddenly the Cat wakes up—still facing away—and yells, "Trap!" The players must drop their arms. If the Mouse is outside the trap, he gets to become the Cat. The old Cat chooses a new Mouse and joins the circle.

If the Mouse is inside when the arms come down, he's caught! The Cat gets to be the Cat again. The caught Mouse chooses a player to be the new Mouse and rejoins the circle.

Variation: With a huge group (fifteen, twenty, or more), half the players can be Mice, and the others form the trap. The first Cat is chosen from the trappers' team. All the mice run in and out, in and out. Round after round, the Cat yells, "Trap!" When all the Mice but one have been caught, the remaining Mouse gets to be the new Cat, and the teams change places.

143

Mulberry Bush

Type: Preschool–kindergarten circle game
Object: Act out the verses in unison
Players: 4 or many more
Ages: 4 and older
Where: Outdoors or in a large room
Equipment: None

Preschoolers get a first taste of group games with Mulberry Bush. All the players join hands and move around in a circle, singing:

> Here we go round the mulberry bush,
>
> mulberry bush, mulberry bush.
>
> Here we go round the mulberry bush,
>
> early in the morning.

The kids stop, release hands, and spin around once.

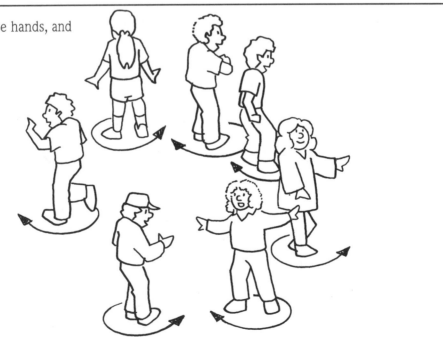

The players then go around in a circle again. This time they take turns suggesting familiar activities, which the whole group sings and acts out. For instance, still standing in the circle, they perform:

This is the way we wash our hands,

wash our hands, wash our hands.

This is the way we wash our hands,

early in the morning.

Then another child chooses an activity:

This is the way we touch our toes,

touch our toes,
touch our toes.

This is the way we touch our toes,

early in the morning.

When everyone has had a turn, the whole group sings and acts out all the activities just once, one after the other, going faster and faster:

This is the way we wash our hands,

This is the way we touch our toes,

This is the way we button our shirt,

This is the way we comb our hair,

This is the way we walk to school,

This is the way we read our books,

This is the way we jump up and down,

Early in the morning.

Around the circle, players help the others by leading the activity they themselves suggested. The round finishes with all the players going round in a circle, singing the first Mulberry Bush verse again.

Musical Chairs

Type: Compete for chairs
Object: Avoid getting left without a seat
Players: 5 plus a monitor, and more is more fun
Ages: 5 and older
Where: Outdoors, gym, or other large room
Equipment: A chair for each player minus 1; a radio or CD/cassette player

To get ready, players gather up a chair for every player, minus one. Five players need four chairs, for example. Place the chairs in a circle, facing toward or away from each other, or line them up in a row, facing alternate directions. (With a really large group, players may arrange the chairs two deep, back to back.)

First, players stand near the chairs, each player an equal distance between two chairs. The monitor starts the music, and the players begin circling.

The monitor suddenly snaps off the music. All the players sit down! Except one, of course—there's one chair too few!

The standing player leaves the game, someone removes one of the chairs, and the music starts again. At the very end, only two players and one chair remain. The one to get the seat wins! If the winner wants, she may serve as monitor next time. Or she may choose someone else to be monitor.

Variation: Preschoolers especially like this less competitive version. Start with one chair per player. At the beginning of each new round of music, remove one chair, but eliminate no players. Each time the music starts, everyone must sit down on a chair somehow! Laughter builds as kids (and grown-ups) squeeze onto four, three, two, and then one chair!

Obstacle Course

Type: Relay race
Object: Be the first team to finish
Players: 4 or more, in teams of 2, 3, or more
Ages: 6 and older
Where: Outdoors, gym
Equipment: A baton (optional); a watch with a second hand or a stopwatch

A big part of the fun for players is building the obstacle course. Players mark a start/finish line and then name fixed objects (climbing gyms, swings, seesaws, trees) or arrange objects (boxes, traffic cones, and so on) in a straight or curving course. The course may be simple or complex, depending on the skill of the players. The racers will have to go around, through, or over the obstacles and, after the last one, run straight back. The challenge may also include *ways* of moving. For instance, the course could require players to climb over the monkey bars, hop down the path, and somersault across the grass. Before beginning, all players should understand the course and know the order in which to tackle the obstacles.

To begin, one team lines up at the start line. With someone keeping time, the first team goes. The first player takes up the baton (or not, if the players decide to race without one), runs the course, returns to the line, and passes the baton. The next player goes. When the last team member finishes, the timekeeper notes how long the team took, and the next team goes. Whichever team finishes the course the fastest wins.

Variation: For a less competitive version, which works well with just a few kids in a wide age range, start by timing each child running the course. Then, challenge each one to beat her own time.

Octopus

Type:	Tag
Object:	Tag and collect players
Players:	6 or more
Ages:	5 and older
Where:	Outdoors, gym
Equipment:	None

The play area is the "ocean," one player is the Octopus, and all the other players are Fish. The Fish line up together on one shore of the ocean. The Octopus stands in the middle of the area and yells, "Swim!" The fish race for the other side, and the Octopus tries to tag them.

As the Octopus tags players, they join hands with him, becoming his tentacles, . . .

. . . and help catch the other Fish in the next rounds. The last player to be caught chooses the Octopus for the next game.

Paper Airplane Race

Type: Plane race
Object: Get over the finish line first
Players: 2 or more
Ages: 5 (with help making planes) and older
Where: Outdoors, gym
Equipment: Paper, paper clips

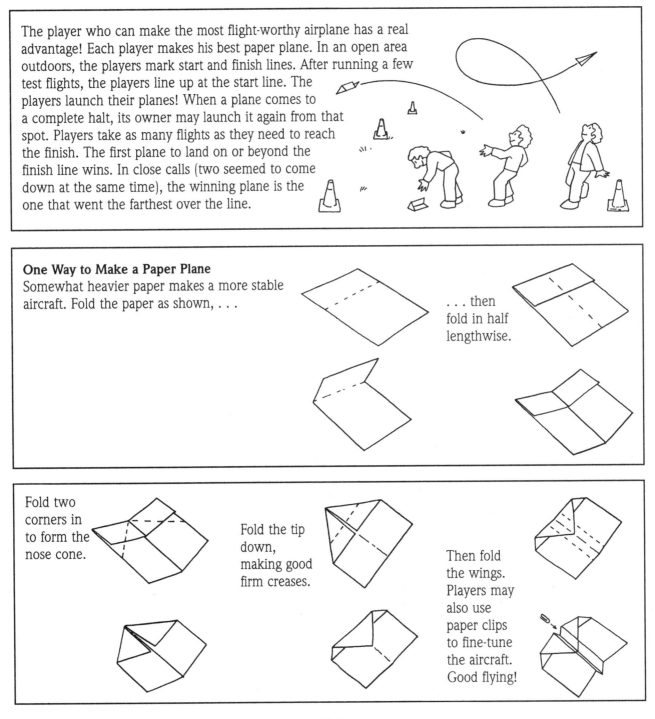

The player who can make the most flight-worthy airplane has a real advantage! Each player makes his best paper plane. In an open area outdoors, the players mark start and finish lines. After running a few test flights, the players line up at the start line. The players launch their planes! When a plane comes to a complete halt, its owner may launch it again from that spot. Players take as many flights as they need to reach the finish. The first plane to land on or beyond the finish line wins. In close calls (two seemed to come down at the same time), the winning plane is the one that went the farthest over the line.

One Way to Make a Paper Plane
Somewhat heavier paper makes a more stable aircraft. Fold the paper as shown, . . .

. . . then fold in half lengthwise.

Fold two corners in to form the nose cone.

Fold the tip down, making good firm creases.

Then fold the wings. Players may also use paper clips to fine-tune the aircraft. Good flying!

150

Pass Ball

Type:	Ball passing
Object:	Keep the balls moving
Players:	6 or more
Ages:	7 and older
Where:	Outdoors, gym
Equipment:	Many balls, up to 1 per player; balls can be alike or very different (a tennis ball, a Nerf ball, a football, a beach ball)

Pass Ball is an exercise in coordination that usually erupts into laughter. Players get in a circle, facing inward. They pile the balls near one player's feet. The player picks up one ball and starts it going around. Once that ball has started its second circuit, the player introduces another ball. After it has made its first circuit, another one is added, and then another. The players pass the balls faster and faster, chanting, "Pass, pass, pass." If someone drops a ball, players should get it back in play as soon as possible. Get a good rhythm going, then go faster and faster until chaos is achieved!

Variation: Large groups can also play in teams. Each team forms a circle. The teams start passing at the same time. The winning team is the one that gets all its balls in play and continues to toss them without a drop for the longest time.

Peanut Race

Type: Race
Object: Get the peanut there first
Players: 2 or more
Ages: 4 and older
Where: Indoors or out
Equipment: Raw or roasted peanuts in the shell, or some other object to push along

Players who are fussy about getting dirty should turn the page now! This simple little race is an exercise in silliness. The players mark start and finish lines. They get down on their knees at the start line. Go! The winner is the first player to push the peanut over the finish line with his chin, nose, or forehead. With peanuts, indoors (carpet or wood floors) may be the best course. Outdoors, players may try using golf balls or alphabet blocks.

Pie Tag

Type: Tag
Object: Avoid getting tagged
Players: 3 or more
Ages: 6 and older
Where: Outdoors, gym
Equipment: Chalk, perhaps

Players draw a six- or eight-piece "pie" (scratched in the dirt or chalked on pavement). They should make it plenty big! To begin, It stands in the middle, and the other players along the edges.

It says, "Go," and goes after a player, trying to tag her. It *and* all the players must run only along the lines of the pie shape.

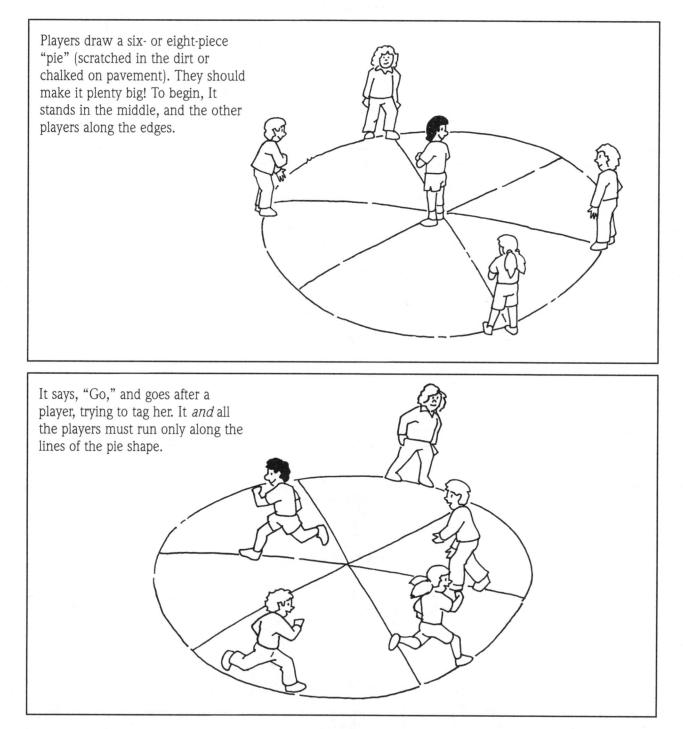

If It tags a player, that player is the new It. Also, if It spots a player running off the lines (each foot must land on a line), that player becomes It.

Players do not have to limit themselves to the pie shape.

They may be creative and draw whatever paths they like.

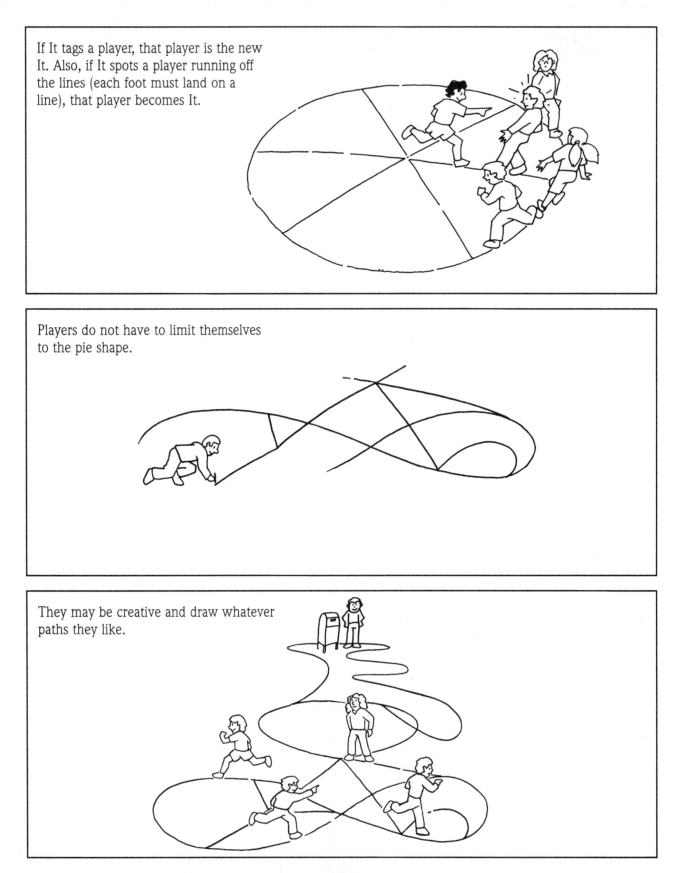

Pig in the Pen

Type: Paper
Object: Finish the most squares
Players: 2–3
Ages: 5 and older
Where: On a car trip or anywhere
Equipment: Paper and pencil

To start, players draw a grid of dots. They may make it with as few dots as the one pictured here or fill a whole page!

One player goes first and draws one line between two adjoining dots.

Players then take turns drawing one line at a time. They may draw up and down (vertically) or side to side (horizontally), but not at a slant (diagonally).

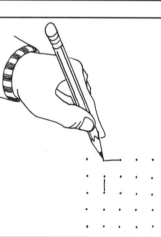

Each player tries to add the fourth side to close up a square. As players draw lines, they try to avoid drawing the third side of square, which will give away the square to the next player in turn. Sooner or later, the grid gets crowded, and someone gets to close a square. Each time a player finishes a square, she puts her own initials inside that square; the pig is in the pen. The player also gets to draw one more line each time she finishes a square.

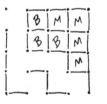

She may take one free turn after another, as long as she finishes up a square on each turn. When all lines have been drawn, the player with the most pigs penned wins.

155

Poison

Type: Tag
Object: Avoid getting tagged
Players: 3 or more
Ages: 5 and older
Where: Outdoors, gym
Equipment: None

At the beginning, It holds out his hands, and each player takes hold of a finger. The players stretch as far away from It as they can while still holding his fingers.

It says, "I went to a shop and bought a bottle of p-p-p-pear juice. I went to a shop and bought a bottle of p-p-p-Pepsi." It continues in this vein, naming a variety of objects that start with *P*. Players may not let go of It's fingers until It says he bought poison. Any player who does is automatically It.

When It finally says "poison," everyone runs!

Now the game becomes just plain Tag. Whoever It tags first is the new It.

Poison Ball

Type: Wacko water un-volleyball
Object: Get the balls into the other court
Players: 2 or many, many more
Ages: 5 (in very shallow water with supervision) and older
Where: In a pool
Equipment: Net or rope, lots of different kinds of balls (at least 1 per player; if only 2 are playing, they should have 3 or 4 balls each), watch with second hand, whistle

Poison Ball is a wacko version of Water Volleyball. The players divide into teams and string a water volleyball net (or just a rope or string of floats) across the playing area. Someone sits on the side to keep time with a second hand. Each player holds the same number of balls (at least one each, but two each is best). When the timekeeper yells, "Go!" the players all start throwing balls into the opposite court.
Whenever a ball lands on their side of the net, the players return it as fast as they can.

After three minutes, the timekeeper blows the whistle, and the throwing stops. Whichever team has fewest balls on its side wins the round! If one team manages to clear all the balls from its court before the ref blows the whistle, it wins the round. Each win is a point. First team with 5 points wins the game.

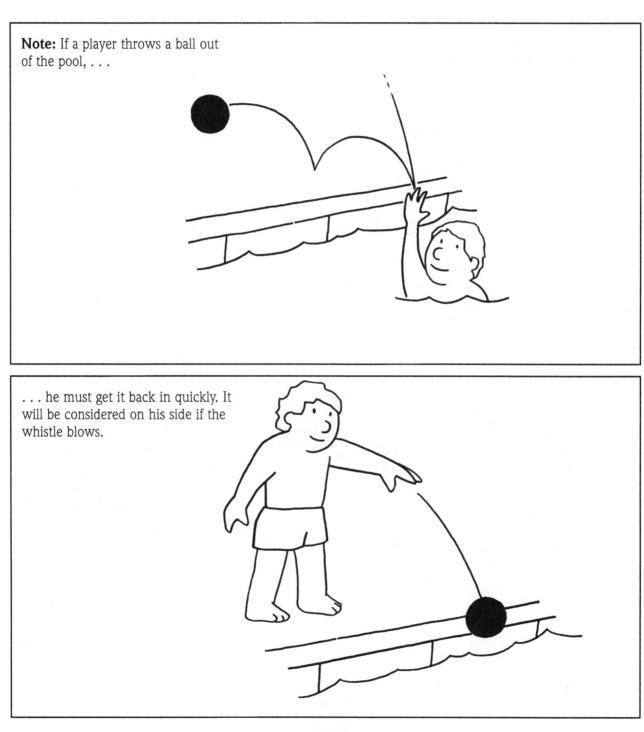

Note: If a player throws a ball out of the pool, . . .

. . . he must get it back in quickly. It will be considered on his side if the whistle blows.

Potato Relay

Type: Relay race
Object: Be the first team to finish
Players: 4 or more
Ages: 5 and older
Where: Outdoors, gym
Equipment: A soupspoon or wooden spoon for each player, a potato for each team

The Potato Relay combines speed and balancing skill. The players divide into teams and mark a start line and a halfway point for a there-and-back race. The teams place their potatoes on the start line, take up their spoons, and line up behind the start line. Go! The first runner for each team lays her spoon on the ground next to the potato, places the potato in it, and lifts the spoon. Now the racers must run to the halfway point and back. If during the race a player drops his potato, he must lay the spoon down and place the potato back in it and pick it up as was done at the start of the race. When they return to the start line, the players must transfer the potato to their teammate's spoon without using their hands. The winning team is the first one to have all its players carry the potato to the halfway point and back.

Prisoner Base

Type: Tag and chase
Object: Put the opponents in jail
Players: 8 or more
Ages: 8 and older
Where: Outdoors, gym
Equipment: None

Players divide into teams and mark out a large rectangular area—thirty by fifty feet is good. The teams mark off "jails" in opposite corners. To start, both jails are empty, and the teams stand in their own courts. Go! The players begin teasing the edges, making runs for each other's empty jails.

There are two ways to put a player in jail: First, if one player reaches his opponents' *empty* jail without being tagged, one of the opponents must go to the opposite jail. The player who pulled this off may go back to his own side untagged.

Second, any player who is tagged in the opponents' territory must go to the opponents' jail.

If some members of a team wind up in the opponents' jail . . .

. . . and a teammate reaches them without getting tagged, they all go free.

But they must be careful as they run back to home court; they can get tagged as they try to escape. The game continues, with everyone making attacks into enemy territory until all the members of one team are in jail. They lose!

Punch Ball

Type: Ball passing
Object: Have fun trying to elude It
Players: 7 or more
Ages: 7 and older
Where: Outdoors, gym
Equipment: Soccer ball or playground ball

Players form a circle and face the inside, standing an arm's length apart. It stays on the outside. To begin, the players hand the ball quickly around the circle. Meanwhile, It runs around, chasing the ball, looking for a chance to punch it into the center as it passes from player to player. The passing players may change the ball's direction at any time and try to fake out It, but they may not throw the ball across the circle. Also, they must hand the ball from player to player, skipping no one and keeping it moving.

When It succeeds in knocking the ball into the center of the circle, the player who was making (not receiving) the pass is the new It. If a player drops the ball, she must get it back into play before It punches it—or she becomes It.

Rabbit

Type:	Tag
Object:	Avoid getting tagged by It
Players:	5 or more
Ages:	6 and older
Where:	Outdoors, gym
Equipment:	None

The players choose a spot for the "rabbit hutch." One player is the Hunter; the others are Rabbits. The Rabbits are safe from the hunter when they're in the hutch. But the Rabbits may not all be in the hutch at one time. One must always be outside, trying to escape the Hunter. To start, the Hunter stands twenty feet away from the hutch, one Rabbit ten feet away, and all the others inside. Go! The Hunter chases the Rabbit who is outside.

If the Rabbit gets to the hutch without being tagged, she's safe. But the first Rabbit she touches . . .

. . . must leave the hutch and run from the Hunter. When the Hunter does tag a Rabbit, the Rabbit becomes the new Hunter. The old Hunter selects a new Rabbit to be outside. The new Hunter and Rabbit take up positions twenty and ten feet away from the hutch, and the game starts again.

Rattlesnake

Type: Group tag
Object: Keep team members' tails away from It
Players: 7 or more
Ages: 6 and older
Where: Outdoors, gym
Equipment: None

The players divide into two or more teams, and the teams form snakes by holding each other's waists. It stands apart. The first player in a line is the snake's Head; the last is the Rattle. Teams start with their Heads pointed at It and their Rattles away. It runs around the snakes, trying to attach to the waist of one of the Rattles. When It connects with a Rattle, the Head of that snake must let go and become It. Every time a team "loses its head," the team gets a point. First team to have 5 points loses.

Red Light, Green Light

Type: Running and stealth
Object: Reach It without being spotted moving
Players: 3 or more
Ages: 5 and older
Where: Outdoors, gym
Equipment: None

It stands facing a tree or wall, so he can't see the other players. Three or more players stand at a start line thirty to fifty feet behind It. It begins by counting *silently* to ten. While It's back is turned, the players move forward. It may count quickly or slowly, but when he finishes, . . .

. . . he shouts, "Red light!" whirling around as he does. Any player It spots moving must go back to the start line. In a couple of seconds, It announces, "Green light," and turns back to count again.

The first player to reach It wins!

Red Rover

Type: Running and strength
Object: Break through the opponents' line
Players: 8 or more
Ages: 5 and older
Where: Outdoors, gym
Equipment: None

The players divide into two teams. The teams line up and face each other at least fifteen feet apart. Team members hold hands tightly. One team calls out the name of an opponent: "Red Rover, Red Rover, send Jack right over." (Teams take turns calling, letting a new player or the same one call it each time.)

Jack leaves his team, . . .

. . . runs over to the opponents' line, and tries to break through their hands.

If Jack breaks through, he gets to pick a player to take with him back to his team. But if he can't break through, he must join that team. The game ends when one team (the winners) has brought over all the members of the other team.

Relay Race (Classic Version)

Type: Race
Object: Be the first team to get there with the baton
Players: 4 or more
Ages: 5 and older
Where: Outdoors, gym
Equipment: A baton, stick, tube, or similar object to relay; the teams should have similar batons

Players establish a racecourse with start and finish lines. The course may be a circle or a long straight line. Either way, mark relay stations along the course—one less than the number of players on each team. For instance, if each team has four members, the course will have three relay stations.

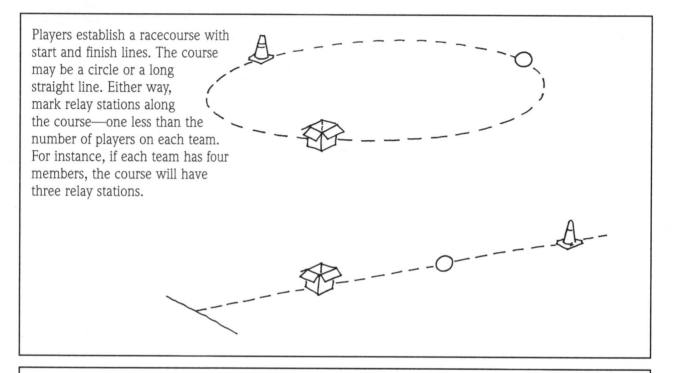

One member of each team stands at the start line, holding the baton, and one stands at each relay station. Go! The starting runner races to station 1 and passes the baton to the runner there, who flies to station 2 and passes the baton to the runner there, and so on until the runner at the last station carries the baton over the finish line. Any runner who drops the baton must pick it up before going on. The first team to get its baton over the finish line wins.

Variation: Another type of course goes from a start line to a midpoint, then back to the start. This course doesn't have relay stations. In this race, all team members line up single file behind the start line. Every runner goes to the midpoint and back to the start line, passing the baton there to the next runner on the team.

Dozens and dozens more variations are around. Many appear elsewhere in this book (Potato Relay, Obstacle Course, Backlash, Ball Duck Race, Jambalaya Relay, Leapfrog, Water Brigade), and players can create infinite varieties with just a little imagination. Players can run relay bicycle races, swim races, skating races, and on and on. To spice things up, the runners may carry all manner of things in place of an ordinary baton: a basketball, a large empty cardboard box, a little red wagon, or anything that can be imagined.

Ring-Around-the-Rosy

Type:	Preschool circle game
Object:	Fun, laughter, learning about group games
Players:	3, 4, or many, many more
Ages:	3 and older
Where:	Outdoors, large room
Equipment:	None

This is the first game many toddlers learn. The youngsters join hands in a circle. They slowly move in a circle, singing:

Ring around the rosy,

Pocket full of posies,

Ashes, ashes, we all fall down.

When they say "down," everyone falls to the ground, laughs, then does it all over.

Rosemary

Type: Ball
Object: Act out something while the ball is in the air
Players: 2 or many more
Ages: 6 and older
Where: Outdoors, gym
Equipment: Rubber playground ball

The players, if more than two, get in a circle. The first player to be It holds the ball and says, "Rosemary is waking up."

Then he tosses the ball up, and . . .

. . . while it is in the air, he acts out waking up (by eye rubbing, yawning, or arm stretching).

Then he catches the ball. The first player tosses the ball to the second and tells that player what Rosemary will do next (eat breakfast, for instance). That player tosses, acts out eating, and catches the ball. The player then passes the ball and an acting assignment to the next player. Players are eliminated for dropping the ball or not acting something out before catching it. They continue until all but one player has been eliminated. The remaining player wins.

Variation: Here's a way to make the game go faster with a large group of players. Each player has a ball. One player is It and gives out the commands every time, as all the other players act them out at the same time. Players are eliminated as they make errors. The last player to survive gets to be the new It.

'Round the World

Type: Pickup basketball
Object: Be first to make all the shots
Players: 2 or more
Ages: 7 and older
Where: A basketball court
Equipment: Basketball hoop and ball

The players mark six or seven spots on a half-court, in a half circle around the basket. To start, the first player shoots from the first spot. If she makes it, she moves to the second spot, shoots from there, and continues around as long as she makes each shot.

When she does miss, she has a choice. She may try again. If she makes it, she may continue on. But if she doesn't make it, she must go all the way back to the beginning.

Her other choice when she misses is to stop where she is and let the other player have his turn. She waits for her next turn to try again, starting from where she left off, rather than being sent back to the start. The winner is the player who first makes all the shots in order, from the first spot through the seventh, *and back*.

Run for Your Supper

Type: Chase and race
Object: Be first to get around the circle
Players: 6 or more
Ages: 5 and older
Where: Outdoors, gym
Equipment: None

Players hold hands in a circle, facing inward. It circles around the outside, tapping players on the shoulders. Suddenly, It taps the joined hands of two players and says, "Run for your supper."

The two players who were tapped leave their places and run around the circle as fast as they can, in opposite directions. Meanwhile, It takes one of their places in the circle.

The first player to make it around the circle fills the gap. There's no place left for the other runner! She's the new It.

Variation: Instead of just saying, "*Run* for your supper," It might say, "Crawl" or "Run backward" or "Skip" or "Hop" or anything else. The players must move exactly the way It orders them.

Safe Tag

Type: Tag
Object: Avoid getting tagged
Players: 3 or more
Ages: 4 and older
Where: Outdoors, gym
Equipment: None

As in basic Tag, the basic action is that It chases the others and tries to tag them. But in Safe Tag, there's a safety zone (any fixed object). Players touching the safety zone cannot be tagged by It; they're safe. To start, all the players are at the safety zone. It tags one of them. That player must leave the safety zone, but It must count to ten before chasing that player.

Other players can choose to take off running, too. It can chase any of them.

If a player gets back to the safety zone and all the other players are there, he tags one of them. That player must leave the safety zone.

Any player tagged by It becomes the new It. The play continues at once.

174

Safety Zones

Type:	Tag
Object:	Avoid getting tagged
Players:	4 or more
Ages:	5 and older
Where:	Outdoors, gym
Equipment:	None

Each player picks a "safety zone." Playground or other fixed equipment is OK, and so are objects placed around by the players. It starts somewhere near the center of the safety zones, and the players stand touching their zones. It waits for someone to let go of the safety zone. Once a player lets go, he or she must next tag up at a different zone. The fun is in challenging It, and soon . . .

. . . a player makes a break for it, leaving his safety zone and racing toward another. The player in *that* safety zone must leave when the other runner arrives . . .

. . . and often will take off for another safety zone when he sees the runner coming. The player in that zone must leave soon, too, since two runners may not occupy the same zone. When a runner leaves a safety zone, the next safety zone he tags must be a *different* one. If It gets between a player and the safety zones, the chase is on! Any player who gets tagged is the new It.

Sardines

Type: Hide-and-seek
Object: Find—and hide with—It
Players: 4 or more
Ages: 6 and older
Where: Outdoors or in a big house
Equipment: None

One player is It. All the others cover their eyes and count. It hides, in a place where the others will eventually be able to join him. When the others finish counting, they start looking for It. They may not team up to look, but must do it on their own.

When a player finds It, he quietly joins him without letting the others see him do it.

When another finds those two, she quietly joins them also.

The last player to find It is the loser. The first one who found It gets to be It next.

Scavenger Hunt

Type: Hunt
Object: Be first to find a series of objects
Players: 3 or more
Ages: 7 and older
Where: Indoors or out
Equipment: Paper, pencils, sacks to carry the collected objects

Scavenger Hunts work best with some sort of leader or host. This individual comes up with a list of objects to find that is fair and fun. The leader doesn't search for the objects. But scavenger hunters could also make up the list together, each contributing the same number of objects. The list should be geared to the amount of time available for the hunt (which could stretch over ten minutes, an hour, or a week), the age of the hunters, and reality. Don't expect to find a snowball in Florida! Once the list has been drawn up, a copy made for each player, and the time limit set, the hunt begins. What happens next will depend on the exact type of hunt the players (or host) have designed. One thing stays the same: the first hunter to find everything on the list wins. (Players should make sure to return belongings to their owners!)

Indoor Scavenger Hunt

If the hunt takes place in one home, the list must be somewhat specialized to that home. However, the hunt won't last long or be much fun if it's too easy. Of course, when hosts design Scavenger Hunts for their own houses, they will know best what will be fun to look for or impossible to find.

Here are some suggestions:

- Several words, phrases, or famous names to find in a stack of old newspapers
- Any insect, live or dead
- A book with a title that contains fifteen different letters
- A paper clip
- A tack
- A toy car
- A stone
- A shell
- A cobweb

Neighborhood Scavenger Hunt

In a neighborhood where several families include kids who are friends, a Scavenger Hunt can fill an entire Saturday and involve a number of households. The best way to do this is to get a parent from each household to contribute items to the list. This list could include fairly ordinary objects such as a ruler, a red shoe, a white saucer, a shell, a knitted cap, the lid to a shoe box, a spool of thread, a rubber band, and a sheet of lined paper. The list can also include some things that are more difficult—but possible—to find.

Yard Scavenger Hunt

Players may also run a totally outdoors, nature-oriented Scavenger Hunt. The list of things to find might include a Y-shaped twig, a centipede, a triangular rock, a four-leaf clover, a pinecone, an acorn, a spider, or whatever might be in the yard or park. Naturally, the list will depend on the season (finding a flower in late winter may be hard, but possible) and the knowledge of the hunters. This is a great activity for a camping trip.

Scissors, Paper, Stone

Type:	Hand and chance
Object:	Choose the dominant hand sign
Players:	2
Ages:	3 and older
Where:	Anywhere
Equipment:	None

Playing Scissors, Paper, Stone is a good way to choose who goes first in two-person games. It's also just plain fun, especially for preschoolers. One round takes about three seconds to play! Players face each other, each holding out one hand in a fist. In unison, the players raise and lower the fists as if banging on a tabletop and say, "One." They do it again and say, "Two." As they do it again and say, "Three," each player brings her hand down either . . .

still in a fist (a stone), in the shape of scissors, or flattened like a piece of paper. Whoever chooses the stronger shape wins. If they choose the same one, they go again until they choose different shapes. But which shape is stronger?

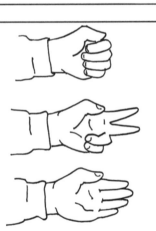

If the players choose . . . the winner is . . . because . . .

If the players choose . . .	the winner is . . .	because . . .
scissors and paper	scissors	scissors cut paper
paper and stone	paper	paper wraps stone
stone and scissors	stone	stone crushes scissors

180

Seven Up

Type: Tossing skill
Object: Successfully perform throwing actions in the right order
Players: 1 or more
Ages: 8 and older
Where: Outdoors or gym, with a throwing wall
Equipment: A rubber playground ball or a bouncy tennis, racquet, or other small ball

Seven Up is a great game for one player to play alone, but more can compete. The player marks a throwing line six or so feet from the wall. From just behind this line, he performs seven different actions, in order. Each action includes throwing the ball, performing some sort of activity, then catching the ball after its first bounce. A player may design the seven activities to suit himself. For instance, to start, he throws the ball against the wall . . .

. . . and catches it.

Next, he throws the ball, twirls once, and catches it. He does this twice.

Third, he bounces the ball, claps once, catches it; throws it, slaps his thighs and claps, then catches; and finally throws, claps, slaps, claps, then catches it.

Fourth, he throws the ball at the wall, claps once in front of his body, claps once behind, and catches it before it bounces. He does this four times.

Next he (five times) throws, slaps his hands on his thighs, does a jumping jack, then catches.

Sixth, he lifts one knee and claps under it, lifts the other knee and claps under it. He does this three times (a total of six claps!).

Finally, he throws the ball with his back to the wall, through his legs, then turns to catch it facing the wall, seven times. The player's goal is to get all the way through this list with no errors. If he makes an error, he must start at the beginning.

Variations: When more than one person play, they may choose one of these variations:

• The players can take turns. If a player makes an error, she stops where she is in the list. When it's her turn again, she resumes at that point. The winner is the one who finishes in the fewest turns.
• Players can also take turns making up actions. A player performs one and then challenges the opponents to perform it as well.

Shadow Tag

Type: Tag
Object: Keep your shadow away from It
Players: 2 or more
Ages: 4 and older
Where: Outdoors in the sunlight; under the floodlights on a summer night
Equipment: None

Like basic Tag, Shadow Tag is a great game for the youngest members of the family. It is especially delightful to four- and five-year-olds. The goal is not to tag another's body, but to step on another's shadow. The players choose an It, who covers his eyes, counts to five, then starts chasing. It shouts, "Gotcha!" when he steps on a player's shadow, and that player immediately becomes It.

Shark and Minnows

Type: Tag
Object: Avoid getting caught by the Shark
Players: 5 or more
Ages: 5 (with supervision) and older in very shallow water; 8 and older for swimmers
Where: In a pool
Equipment: None

First, the players decide on the boundaries of the game—that is, how much of the pool to use. One player, the Shark, stands or treads water in the center of this area. The other players, the Minnows, line up together on one side. The shark yells, "Swim!" or, "Go!" The Minnows jump in (or dive into deeper water, if allowed) and head for the opposite side (or the rope, if it is the opposite boundary), where they will be safe.

The Shark goes after the Minnows and tries to tag them. The Shark may tag more than one of them in a round. Any Minnow that gets tagged . . .

. . . must join up with and help the Shark. The round ends when all the Minnows have reached the opposite side or been tagged. The next round begins with any tagged Minnows and the Shark in the center of the playing area, ready to tag the remaining Minnows. Rounds are played until only one Minnow has survived. That Minnow gets to pick out the next Shark.

184

Sheep, Sheep, Come Home

Type: Chase and tag
Object: Run across the area without getting tagged
Players: 6 and more
Ages: 5 and older
Where: Outdoors, gym
Equipment: In a gym, the Wolf needs something to crouch behind (bushes work well outdoors)

One player is the Shepherd, one the Wolf, and all the others are Sheep. The Shepherd gathers all the Sheep in a group, then goes to the other side of the play area. Somewhere in between is the Wolf, who crouches and hides. The Shepherd calls out, "Sheep, sheep, come home!" and they run across to him.

When they get near, the Wolf springs out. When the Wolf catches (tags) a Sheep, he puts it in his den (the spot where he was crouching) until the end of the game. All the others race to get behind the Shepherd. When all the Sheep are either in the den or behind the Shepherd, the round ends.

Rounds are played until only one Sheep is left. She gets to be either the Wolf or the Shepherd, and she chooses a player for the other role in the next game.

Shopping Trip

Type: Memory game
Object: Remember the shopping list the best
Players: 2–10 or more
Ages: 8 or older
Where: On a car trip or anywhere
Equipment: None

One player starts by saying, "I went to the grocery store and bought **A**pple cider" (or some other word beginning with *A*). The second adds an item beginning with *B*: "I went to the grocery store and bought **A**pple cider and **B**read." The next player adds a *C* word: **A**pple cider, **B**read, and **C**andy. As each player's turn comes around, he or she must add an item to the list in alphabetical order. Players must remember and repeat every item, then add their own. A player who makes a memory mistake is out. The last remaining player wins. If there's more than one winner, great!

Sidewalk Golf

Type: Homemade putt-putt
Object: Hit the targets, avoid the hazards
Players: 2 or more
Ages: 7 and older
Where: Outside
Equipment: A marker (stone, penny, or milk cap) and chalk

In a paved area, each player designs a "hole." A hole is not just the opening that the ball rolls into, but everything that leads up to and surrounds that opening. All the holes together make up the course. In designing a hole, each player draws the target hole itself (about the size of a baseball) and, in a large area around it, hazards like alligator ponds and sand traps. At the far side from the target hole is a teeing line, where players must stand to start the hole.

The players go through the course together. First one player tosses a marker at each hole until she reaches the target hole. If the player lands in a hazard, she must take back her marker, and she starts again from the teeing line. If she lands outside the target hole but not in a hazard, she tries again from where she landed. When her marker lands in the target hole, the other player takes his turn at that hole. Then both move on to the next hole. A player gets 1 point for each attempt. When each player has played each hole, they total their points. Low score wins.

Variation: Players can also use a graveled area, shaping the hazards with gravel, or under pine trees, using the pine straw.

Simon Says

Type:	Follow the leader
Object:	Do only what Simon says
Players:	2 or more
Ages:	4 and older
Where:	Indoors or (more actively) out
Equipment:	None

One player is Simon. All the others line up in front of Simon, and Simon begins to give out orders. At first, all orders start with "Simon says . . . ." The players must do whatever Simon says, but only if he uses the words *Simon says*. Simon's instructions may be anything within reason: stand on one foot . . . hop up and down . . . stand on "all fours" backward.

Eventually, Simon gives an order without the *Simon says*: "Touch your nose." If a player touches her nose, she's out! Play continues until only one player is left. That player is Simon next.

Simon Says *Not*

Type: Don't follow the leader
Object: Do not do what Simon says
Players: 2 or more
Ages: 7 and older
Where: Indoors or (more actively) out
Equipment: None

This is Simon Says for stubborn, willful players. As with Simon Says, one player is Simon, and the others line up. Then Simon begins giving out orders. But instead of following directions when they hear "Simon says," the players do just the opposite. For example, if Simon says to hold out a right hand, the players hold out their left hands. If he says the players must cover their heads with their left hands, the players cover with their right. Or if Simon says to breathe, they hold their breath.

Also, if Simon gives a command without the words *Simon says*, the players *should do* as they are directed. Simon's got quite a job. He must give commands that have an opposite and watch carefully to catch an error. Even Simon can get confused. One mistake, and a player is out. Last player to be in is Simon next time.

Skate Obstacle Course

Type: Race
Object: Make it through the obstacles first
Players: 2 or more
Ages: Able to roller-skate
Where: An open paved area (a long driveway is perfect)
Equipment: Roller skates, miscellaneous obstacles

Players mark a starting line and get together some obstacles—milk jugs, boxes, small trash cans, whatever is on hand. They arrange the obstacles on a straight or curving course and decide how players must circle the obstacles and in what order. The goal is to complete the course on roller skates in the shortest time possible. Players must also decide whether the skater must simply make it past the last obstacle or go around the last obstacle then race straight back to the start line.

Variation: Race the course on bikes.

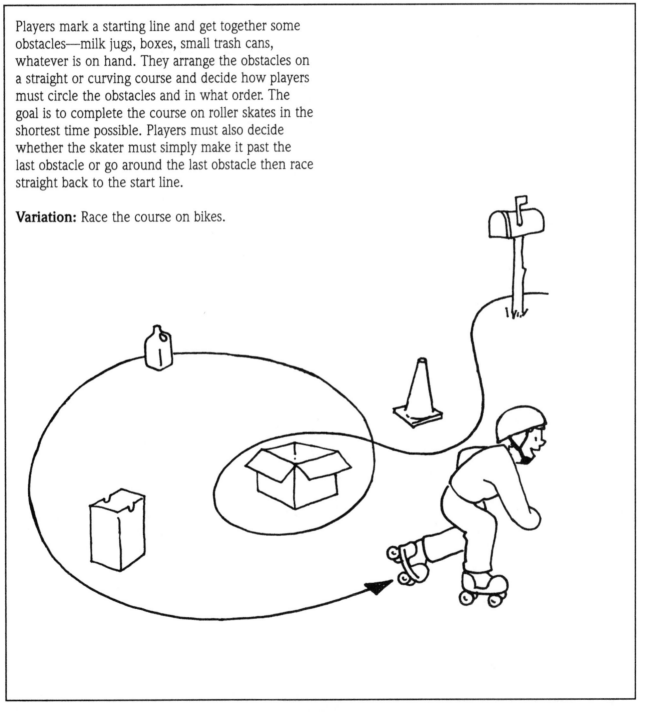

Soccer Tag

Type: Ball tag
Object: Avoid being tagged
Players: 3 or many more
Ages: 8 and older
Where: Outdoors, gym
Equipment: Soccer ball or rubber playground ball

The players set boundaries for a large play area. Each player starts out with 3 points. A player is chosen to be It. It takes the ball, goes outside a boundary, puts the ball down, and kicks it into the playing area.

Then other players dodge and run, and It goes after them, trying to tag them with a *kick* of the ball. Each time a player is tagged, the player loses a point and becomes It. If a player loses all 3 points, she's out. (On losing her third, she chooses a player to be It next. Players don't lose points when *chosen* to be It.) The last player to survive wins.

Spell It How? (Llep Stiw Oh?)

Type: Word
Object: Figure out the backward word
Players: 2 or more
Ages: 9 and older
Where: In the car or anywhere
Equipment: Paper and pencil (optional)

One player is It. It thinks of an easy-to-spell object: igloo. She says it out loud *backward*: "Oolgi." (To be fair, players shouldn't change the way the vowels sound.) Now the other player(s)—either in their heads or on paper—try to figure out the word. The first player to get it right is It next. If no one can guess, It tells the answer and goes again. Highly literate players may try using whole phrases, which can be quite hard. They will almost certainly want to use paper and pencil to help with solutions.

Spoons

Type: Card
Object: Avoid getting stuck without a spoon
Players: 4–12
Ages: 7 and older
Where: On the floor or at the table
Equipment: Spoons and a deck of playing cards

The game of Spoons guarantees a fall-down-laughing good time. Players get some spoons, one fewer than the number of players, then sit in a circle on the floor or around a table. The spoons are placed in the center, handles pointing out, equally close to all players. The dealer gives each player four cards and piles the remaining ones facedown on her left. She then picks a card from the pile and decides whether to keep it. She (like the other players) is looking for four cards alike (four twos, four kings, and so on). She discards one of her cards facedown on her right.

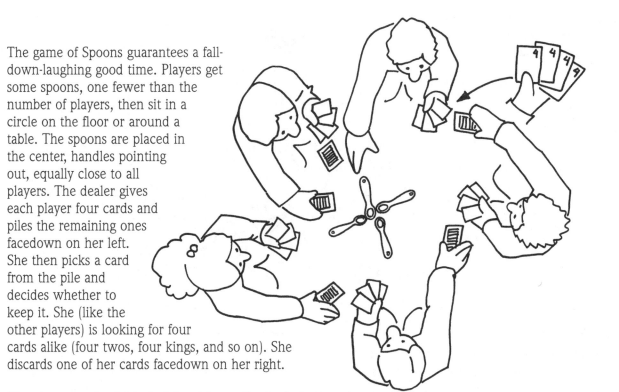

The player on the dealer's right picks up the dealer's discard, decides whether to keep it, and puts one facedown on his right. Around the table, players furiously pick up and discard, never holding more than four in their hands and always trying to complete a set of four. When the dealer has used up the pile, she begins picking up discards from the player to her left.

When one player gets four of a kind, he quietly takes a spoon. If no one notices, he may keep passing cards (without bothering to look at the new one!).

Any player who notices the taken spoon may also take a spoon (without needing four of a kind). Since there aren't enough spoons for everyone, there's a mad scramble at the end! The player without a spoon gets the letter *S*, and the game begins from the beginning. The next time the same player doesn't get a spoon, she gets the letter *P*. The first player to spell SPOONS loses.

Spud

Type: Ball tag
Object: Avoid being tagged
Players: 5 or more
Ages: 6 and older
Where: Outdoors, gym
Equipment: Rubber playground ball

One player (It) tosses the ball up and calls another player's name. The player whose name is called becomes the new It.

Everyone else runs, while It stays to catch the ball. Once It has the ball, he shouts, "Spud!" Everyone stops running.

It may now take three giant steps in any direction. (Or, before starting, players may decide to allow a different number of steps.) It stops and throws the ball at a player. If he hits the player, the player gets the letter *S* and becomes It. If It misses, *he* gets the *S* and is It again.

The first player to get four letters—*S, P, U, D*—loses and must become It.

Squareball

Type:	Dodgeball
Object:	Tag the opponents
Players:	8 or more
Ages:	8 and older
Where:	Paved area, driveway, outdoor basketball or tennis court
Equipment:	Rubber playground ball

The players divide into two teams and draw the court shown. The length of the sides and number of bases depend on the number of players. There should always be four corner bases; add a side base for every additional team member.

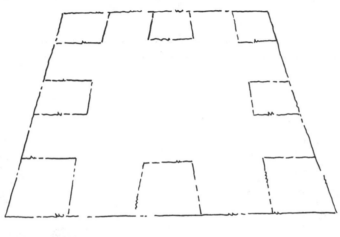

The players on one team stand in the bases. (If there's an odd player—say, eight members on one team, nine on the other—two players can share one of the bases.) The other team huddles in the middle of the court. To begin, the team players on the bases throw the ball quickly among themselves, back and forth or round and round the square—but not across the square. Suddenly, a base player takes a shot at an inner player. If an inner player is hit, . . .

. . . all the base players flee the court. The hit player goes after the ball.

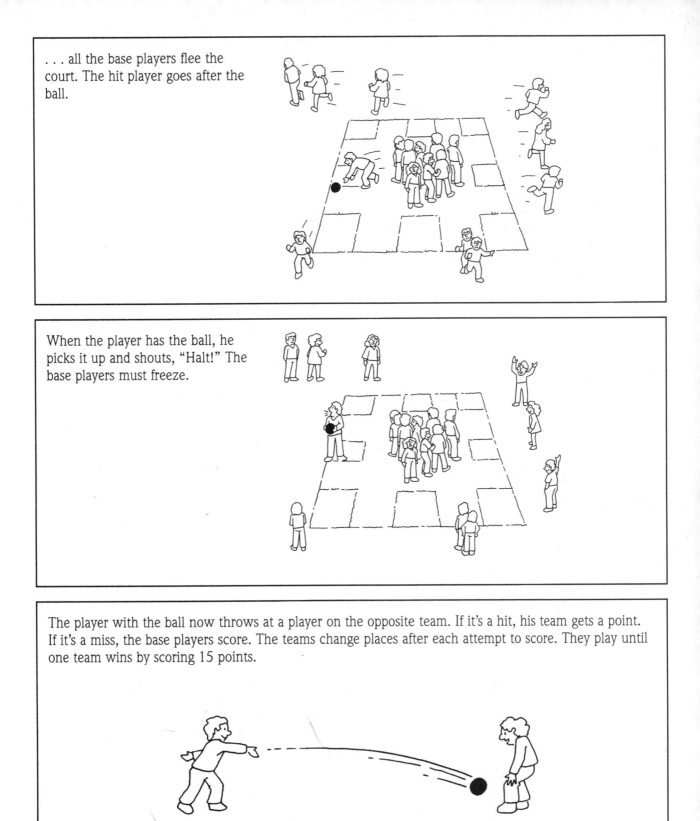

When the player has the ball, he picks it up and shouts, "Halt!" The base players must freeze.

The player with the ball now throws at a player on the opposite team. If it's a hit, his team gets a point. If it's a miss, the base players score. The teams change places after each attempt to score. They play until one team wins by scoring 15 points.

Statues

Type: Flinging players
Object: Show off dramatic flair
Players: 4 or more
Ages: 5 and older
Where: Outdoors, gym
Equipment: None

One player is It. To start, It names an activity: flying, basketball, sleeping, boxing, anything. It then takes a player by the hand and whirls him around. (It may whirl so hard that the player's feet leave the ground. If so, they should be playing on soft grass!) Suddenly, It lets go.

The flung player must land in some pose related to the activity named by It. But he must stop naturally when the force of the throw ends. It can disqualify a player for putting extra movement into a landing. Players hold their poses until everyone has been flung.

When all the players have been flung, It decides who has struck the best pose. That player is the next It.

Tag

Type: Basic tag
Object: Chase and tag opponents
Players: 2 or more
Ages: 4 and older
Where: Outdoors, gym
Equipment: None

Basic Tag is very simple. One player is It. It chases the other players. When It tags someone, the tagged player gets out of the game. The last player to survive is the winner.

Variation: The tagged player may instantly become It. Play continues endlessly, every tagged player immediately becoming It.

Teacher's Cat

Type: Word
Object: Think of things in alphabetical order
Players: 2 or more
Ages: 8 and older
Where: On a car trip or anywhere
Equipment: None

First, each player must describe the teacher's cat with a word that starts with *A*. The first player says, "The teacher's cat is angry," the second, "The teacher's cat is asleep," and so on. When all players have thought of an *A* word for the cat, the first player goes again, this time thinking of a *B* word: black, bossy, or Burmese. They continue taking turns through each letter of the alphabet. No words may be repeated. When a player's turn arrives, he must speak without hesitation. If he pauses, he's out (or gets a point). Players take turns going first (last can be the hardest position) but should play every round in the same order. Players may play for elimination. (The player who pauses too long or gives up is out; the last player to survive wins.) Or players may compete with points. (A player gets a point for pausing or giving up; the player with the low score in the end wins.)

Telephone Message

Type:	Word whispering
Object:	Have fun discovering how the message changes
Players:	4–dozens
Ages:	5 and older
Where:	Anywhere
Equipment:	None

The players sit in a circle. The first player thinks up a short message ("The yellow tree fell on the house," for instance), then whispers it in the ear of the next player so no one else can hear. That player then whispers the message to the next, and the message travels on around the circle until it reaches the last player. A player may whisper the message only once. No matter how odd the message sounds to the listening player, the listener must do the best she can to pass real words on to the next player. When the message has gone full circle, the last player says it out loud. Then the first player reveals the original message. "The yellow tree fell on the house" may become "Hey, you—those three bells scared the mouse!" Sometimes not a single word from the original survives the trip!

Tell a Tale

Type: Word
Object: Have fun seeing the original tale change
Players: Large group (10 at least)
Ages: 6 and older
Where: Anywhere
Equipment: None

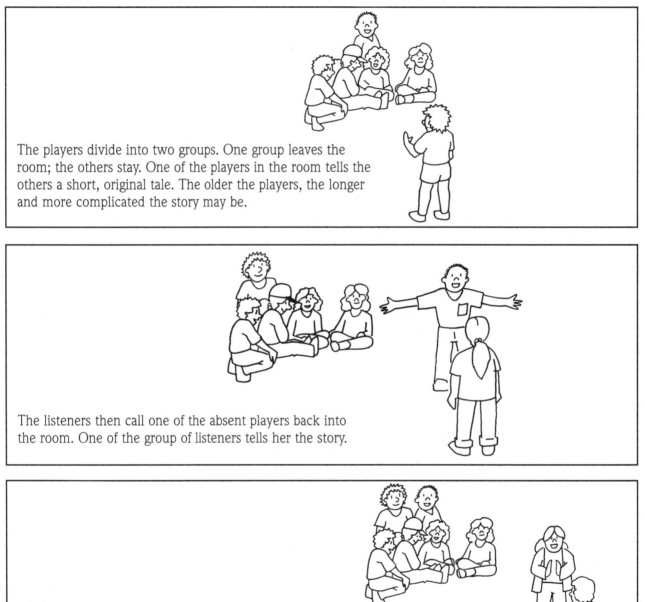

The players divide into two groups. One group leaves the room; the others stay. One of the players in the room tells the others a short, original tale. The older the players, the longer and more complicated the story may be.

The listeners then call one of the absent players back into the room. One of the group of listeners tells her the story.

She, in turn, retells the story to *another* returning player. One by one, players return and are told the story by the one who last heard it. The players who never left the room enjoy this game the most. They laugh uproariously—to the puzzlement of the tellers—as the story changes completely!

Three Words

Type: Word
Object: Enjoy the players' different ways of seeing things
Players: 2 or more
Ages: 5 and older
Where: On a car trip or anywhere
Equipment: None

This game has no winners or losers. Five-year-olds are as good as (or better than) fifty-year-olds. One player (It) names three nouns: *bird, airplane, cat.* The other players take turns answering the question, Which two things go together, and which is different?

One answer: A cat and a bird are alive; an airplane isn't.

Another player might say that birds and airplanes fly, but cats don't. The fun is in how different the answers are!

Variation: For a more competitive version, there is only one right answer (It's answer), and It is allowed to be tricky. For instance, the words *bird* and *cat* both start with consonants, *airplane* with a vowel. It listens as the others take turns offering solutions.

The first player to come up with It's answer is It next time.

Throw and Go

Type:	Ball toss-and-run drill
Object:	Keep things going fast—an exercise in speed and coordination
Players:	6–20
Ages:	8 and older
Where:	Outdoors, gym
Equipment:	Rubber playground ball or other easy-to-catch ball

The players stand in two lines, several feet apart. The first player in one line throws the ball to the first player in the other line.

The player who threw the ball then runs to the end of his line. The player who caught the ball throws it to the (now first) player in the other line . . .

. . . and runs to the end of his line. This continues, with the ball going faster and faster and with no pausing between catch, throw, and Go! The action keeps going until every player has changed lines—or everyone is totally tangled up!

Thumb
Wrestling

Type: Test of thumb strength
Object: Put down the opponent's thumbs
Players: 2
Ages: 5 and older
Where: On a tabletop
Equipment: None

It's not that important in Thumb Wrestling if the opponents aren't equal in overall strength and size. Each player lays a forearm on the tabletop, and they clasp hands as shown, thumbs up.

On the count of three, they lower their thumbs and press them side to side, trying to press each other's thumbs back. The player who presses her opponent's thumb back wins. Players may play three out of five or five out of seven for a champ.

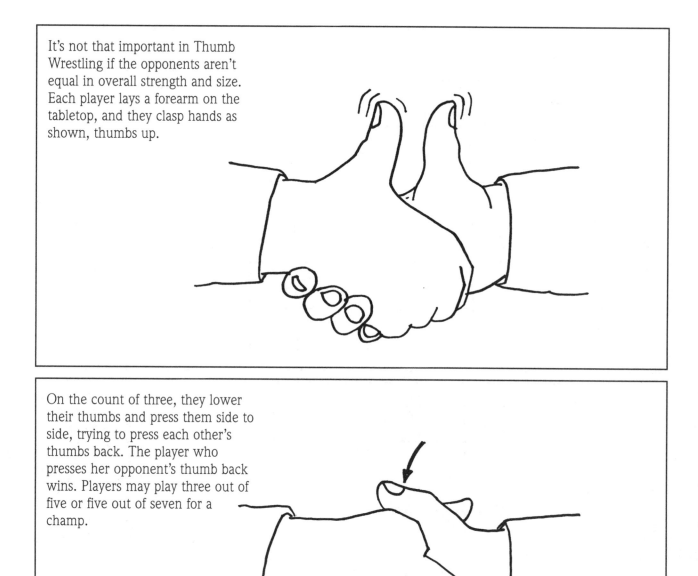

Tic-Tac-Toe

Type: Paper
Object: Be first to mark three squares in a row
Players: 2
Ages: 4 and older
Where: On a car trip or anywhere
Equipment: Paper and pencil

Games don't get simpler than Tic-Tac-Toe! Draw the grid as shown. One player is X, the other is O.

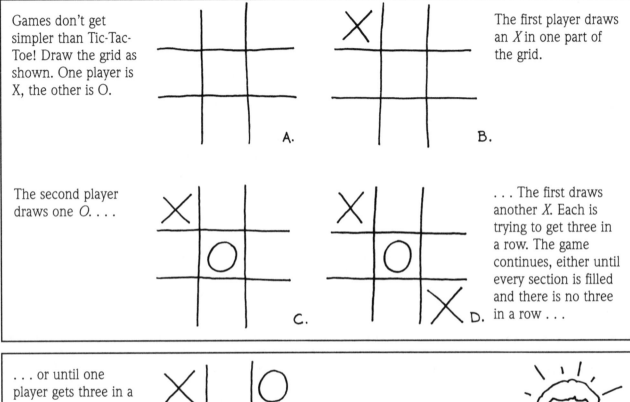

A.

B.

The first player draws an X in one part of the grid.

The second player draws one O. . . .

C.

D.

. . . The first draws another X. Each is trying to get three in a row. The game continues, either until every section is filled and there is no three in a row . . .

. . . or until one player gets three in a row and wins. Players usually play many games in a row, getting a point per win. The higher scorer at the end wins.

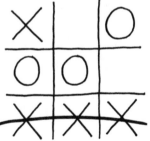

Variation: Players use the same kind of grid and take turns, one making *X*s, the other *O*s. However, the players try to *not* get three in a row. The player who does, loses.

Tic-Tac-Toe Four

Type: Paper
Object: Get four *X*s or *O*s in a row
Players: 2
Ages: 5 and older
Where: On a car trip or anywhere
Equipment: Paper, pencil, ruler

This is a sort of combination of Pig in the Pen and Tic-Tac-Toe. Graph paper is handy, but players can easily draw their own grid, as shown. Just as with Tic-Tac-Toe, one player draws *X*s, the other *O*s. They take turns drawing them one at a time. However, in Tic-Tac-Toe Four, the first player with *four* marks in a row wins. Good luck!

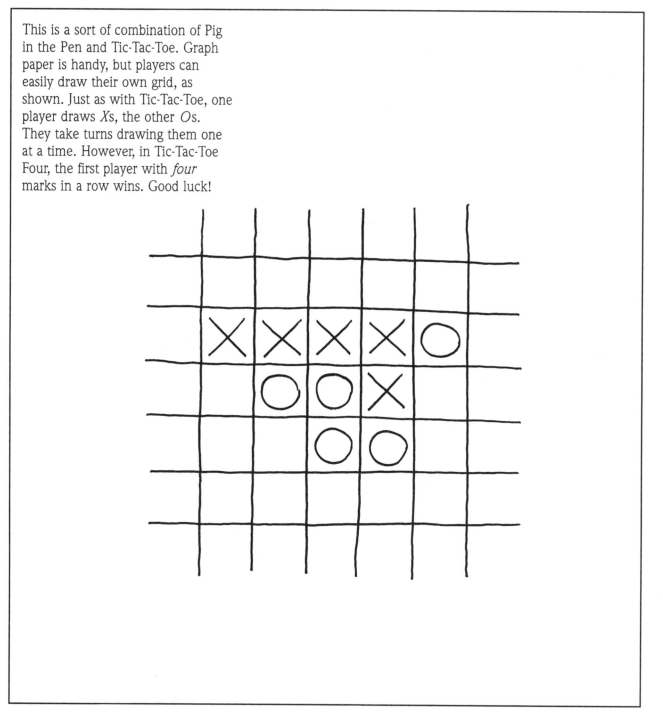

Toss Ball

Type: Catching and throwing
Object: Avoid making errors and stay in the game
Players: 4 or more
Ages: 7 and older
Where: Outdoors, gym
Equipment: A small, softish ball, beanbag, or Koosh ball

One player is It. It stands ten or more feet in front of the other players, who are seated in a row. To start, It calls out a player's name and tosses the ball straight at her.

It must now twirl around once. The named player must stand, catch the ball, . . .

throw it straight back to It, and sit before It catches the ball. During all this, there are several ways for It or the player to be eliminated: If the player throws the ball fairly back to It but he isn't ready or misses, It is eliminated. If It fails to twirl or throws wild, he's eliminated. (If It is eliminated, he gets to choose a new It.) If the named player catches the ball while still seated, fails to catch it, throws it while sitting, or throws it wild, she's eliminated. If none of these things happen, It and the called player switch places, and another round begins. The last player to survive is the winner.

Tree Ball

Type: Ball tag
Object: Avoid getting tagged
Players: 3 or more (up to the number of trees in the area)
Ages: 7 and older
Where: Outdoors
Equipment: Rubber playground or soccer ball; trees

One player is It. All the other players claim trees and use them as shields. It has the ball.

It tries to kick the ball and hit the other players.

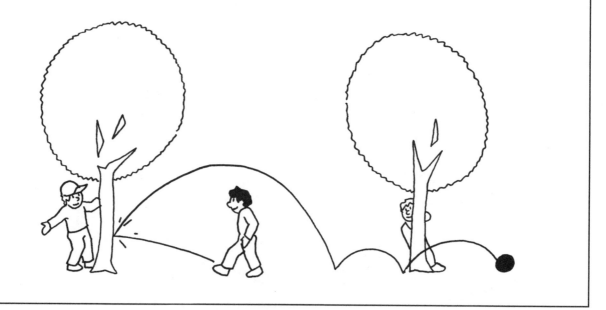

209

Players run from tree to tree, teasing It and forcing each other to move (only one player is allowed per tree at a time).

If It manages to tag a player with the ball, It then claims an unoccupied tree. The tagged player becomes It.

Variation: Players may also play with a beanbag or other soft object and throw instead of kick.

Trips

Type: High-speed throwing and catching
Object: Be the first team to finish the round
Players: 6–21 (at least 2 teams of 3 players each)
Ages: 8 and older
Where: Outdoors, gym
Equipment: Tennis or racquet balls, or baseballs and gloves

Players divide into three-member teams. A team's three players—first, center, and third—stand in a line with at least fifteen feet between them. The center player starts by throwing the ball to the first player. All teams must make the first throws at the same time.

The first player catches the ball and throws it *over* the center player to the third player, . . .

. . . who returns it to the first player over the center. The players should throw fast. However, a dropped ball, which must be returned to play from where it was dropped, will slow them down.

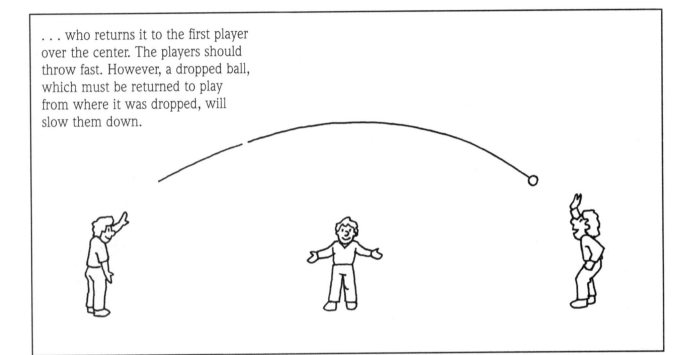

The first player then completes the first "trip" by throwing the ball back to the center player. At the end of the first trip, the team calls out, "One!" and at the end of the second trip, "Two!" and so on. Play immediately continues. The first team to finish ten trips wins.

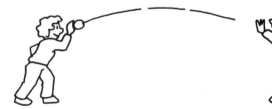

Trips, Jr.

Type: Throwing and catching
Object: Be the first team to finish the round
Players: 6–21 (at least 2 teams of 3 players each)
Ages: 5 and older
Where: Outdoors, gym
Equipment: A rubber playground ball

Divide into teams of three players—first, center, and third. The three players on one team line up with five or six feet between them. The center player starts by throwing the ball to the first player, who catches it. All teams must make the first throw at the same time.

The first player rolls the ball through the center's legs to the third player.

The third player returns it to the
first player—again through the
center's legs.

The first player throws the ball back to the center,
completing the "trip." As they complete each trip, players
call out, "One trip, "Two trips," and so on. The first team
to finish five trips wins.

Tug-of-War

Type: Contest of strength
Object: Outpull the opponents
Players: 6 or more
Ages: 4 and older
Where: Outdoors (a soft, grassy area is best) or gym
Equipment: A long, smooth, thick rope—not a cord—(old sheets with knots for handholds work well)

The players divide into two teams of fairly equal strength. The teams line up single file on either side of a line. The teams hold opposite ends of the rope, everyone keeping a firm hold. Go! They pull with all their might.

The object is to pull the other team over the center line. When one team member steps over the line, that team loses.

Variation: In summer, play Tug-of-War with the rope over a wading pool. The object? Pull the opponents into the water!

215

Twenty Questions

Type: Guessing
Object: Guess what It is thinking of
Players: 2 or more
Ages: 7 and older
Where: On a car trip or anywhere
Equipment: None

One player is It. It thinks of an object, then tells the others whether the object is animal (including dead or living insects, reptiles, and birds), vegetable (plant matter, whether alive or dead—wood, for instance), or mineral (anything natural or man-made that's never been alive). The other players take turns asking questions about the object. They may ask about size, color, whether it is made by people or is a part of nature—but they can only ask a total of twenty questions. Also, It must be able to answer each question with a simple yes or no. Twenty Questions may be played for the fun of it, with the players taking turns being It. Or it may be played for score: anytime an It picks an object no one can guess, he or she gets a point and gets to be It again. If a player does guess the object, that player gets a point and gets to be It. First player to have 5 points wins.

Twenty-One

Type: Pickup basketball
Object: Be first to make all the shots
Players: 2
Ages: 8 and older
Where: A basketball court
Equipment: Basketball hoop and ball

To start, the first player stands at the foul line and shoots. The other player waits under the basket.

If the first player makes the shot, she gets a point. The other player returns the ball, and the first player tries again, shooting again and again each time she makes the shot.

If she misses, she *and* her opponent try to get the rebound. . . .

. . . Whoever gets it may make a layup shot (a shot from right under the basket). The players now just play two-person basketball, keeping the ball in play by dribbling and shooting. As soon as someone either makes a shot or knocks the ball out of bounds, the ball is taken to the foul line for shooting by the player who made the shot or did not knock the ball out of bounds. This player gets to take one shot after another, just as the first player did, as long as she makes the shot. The game is over when one player wins by scoring 21 points.

Ultimate Frisbee

Type: A sort of soccer, with Frisbees
Object: Move the Frisbee across the goal line and score
Players: 6 or more
Ages: 8 and older
Where: Outdoors in a *big* open area
Equipment: Frisbee

Form two teams. Mark goal lines at opposite ends of the playing area. The size of the area should be determined by the age and skill of the players. One team gets behind each line. To start, a member of one team tosses the Frisbee to the other team (the receivers), and the whole team runs toward the receivers. The receivers may catch the thrown Frisbee or pick it up from where it falls to the ground.

The receivers try to make a goal by moving the Frisbee to their own goal line (the line from which it was thrown). The only way to move it is for one team member to throw to another, who catches it and throws it to another. The team that started play (the defenders) tries to stop the receivers from making a goal. They try to intercept the Frisbee or bat it to the ground. If their team gets the Frisbee, they immediately try to move it to the opposite goal line. The team that gets the Frisbee over its goal line scores a point. For the team to score, a team member must catch the Frisbee on the other side of the line; the team can't just throw it over the line. After a score, the teams immediately change roles (throwers become the receivers and vice versa) for the next try.

Official Ultimate Frisbee has turned into a serious sport! It has detailed and specific rules. For a friendly game, though, these basics should do:

Players may move the Frisbee only by passing. They may not run with the Frisbee in hand. If a player is caught running or walking while holding the Frisbee, the team must turn over the Frisbee to the other team.

Players must pivot on only *one* foot while holding or throwing. They may not take a foot-to-foot step.

A team may not gang up on an opponent who has the Frisbee. Only one defender may guard that player.

If someone on the receiving team misses or fumbles the Frisbee during passing and it hits the ground, the Frisbee goes to the other team.

If a player standing out of bounds catches the Frisbee, it goes to the other team.

Play stops when someone scores. To score, one player *on the field* throws the Frisbee to a team member *over the goal line*. The team member who catches it may have been standing past the goal line waiting or may have run there just in time. If the Frisbee goes over the line and lands on the ground, it goes to the other team who starts back with it to their goal.

Underwater Tag

Type: Tag
Object: Avoid being tagged by It
Players: 3 or more
Ages: Old enough to swim underwater
Where: In a pool
Equipment: None

As in basic Tag, It chases the other players and tries to tag them. As in some other versions of Tag, the players can be safe from being tagged by being in a certain place. In Underwater Tag, that place is *underwater*! It may not tag any player who has his complete body underwater. Once safely underwater, players should swim away fast. While It might give up and go after someone else, she also might follow and wait for the underwater player to surface. If tagged, the player becomes It, and the game continues immediately.

Virginia Woolf

Type: Guessing
Object: Stump the other players with a hard name
Players: 2 or more
Ages: 10 and older
Where: On a car trip or anywhere
Equipment: None

One player is It. It thinks of a famous person. The person may be dead or alive but must be famous enough to be known by everyone in the group. (It's OK if, instead of famous, the person is just someone that everyone in the group knows—for instance, a teacher or neighbor.) It says, "I am thinking of someone whose name begins with the letter *W*" (or whatever the first letter of the person's last name). The other players take turns guessing the person's name by asking questions about the person. These must be questions that It can answer with a yes or a no. The guessers may ask up to a total of twenty questions. The game may be played for the fun of it, with the players just taking turns being It. Or the game may be played for score: the players take turns being It and may score only while they are It. They get a point for thinking of a (fair) name that no one can guess. First player to score 3 points wins.

Volcano

Type: Chase and keep a place
Object: Find a spot when the clapping stops
Players: Large group (10 at least)
Ages: 8 and older
Where: Outdoors, gym
Equipment: None

One player is It. He stands apart. The others stand in two circles, one inside the other. Each player in the outer circle stands exactly behind a player in the inner circle. It shouts, "Volcano!" then starts clapping.

The outer players begin running around in all directions. The inner players "erupt" by clapping and roaring! The outer players keep circling until It stops clapping and takes a spot behind a player in the inner circle. This is the signal for the inner players to stop clapping and for each runner to find a place behind an inner player. But It has taken a spot, so there's one place too few. The player who can't find a place becomes It, and the inner and outer players change places.

Volleyballoon

Type: Volleyball-like, but with balloons
Object: Volley and don't let the balloon hit the ground
Players: 2 or more
Ages: 6 and older
Where: Outdoors, gym, large indoor space
Equipment: Air-filled balloons

For four or more players, the players divide into teams. Players tie a string or net between two trees, chairs, or whatever is at hand. Opponents try to bat the balloon with their hands back and forth across the net. Each team may touch the balloon only three times before getting it over the net. At all costs, they must keep the balloon off the floor or ground! If the balloon comes down on one side, the other player or team gets a point. First to score 10 points wins.

Variation: For a more challenging game, the balloon is not even allowed to fall below net level.

Wall of China

Type: Chase and tag
Object: Cross the "wall" without getting tagged
Players: 9 or more
Ages: 6 and older
Where: Outdoors, gym
Equipment: None

Players mark two lines, five or six feet apart, as long as needed for the number of players. This is the "wall." One player (or two for a huge group) stands on the wall. This person is the tagger and must stay on the wall. The others line up on one side.

The runners start crossing the wall at will, going back and forth as many times as they can. Players earn a point every time they cross without getting tagged. Once a player has been tagged, she is out. When all the players have been tagged out, the player with the highest score is the winner and gets to choose the next tagger(s).

War

Type: Card
Object: Play the higher of two cards
Players: 2–4
Ages: 4 (if playing with an adult) and older
Where: Anywhere
Equipment: Deck of playing cards

Card games don't get any simpler than War! Players deal out the entire deck of cards. Each player keeps his cards facedown in a pile in front of him. To start, each player turns his top card faceup. The player with the highest card takes all the played cards and puts them facedown in the bottom of his pile. (If the jokers are included, they have the highest value.) If there's a tie, each of the tying players turns one more card up. The one who played the highest second card takes all the cards from both plays. Play continues until someone runs out of cards. The winner is then the player who has the most cards or play goes for five minutes, and the winner is the player with the most cards at the end of that time.

War Times Two

Type: Card
Object: Play the highest two cards
Players: 2–4
Ages: 5 (if playing with an adult) and older
Where: Anywhere
Equipment: Deck of playing cards; a watch (optional)

War Times Two is basically played like War, but the players turn over two cards at a time. The winner of each round is the player whose two cards add up to the most points. Kings, queens, and jacks are worth 10 points, aces 11, and jokers 12. This makes it easier to get an opponents' high cards, since an ace and a two (for example) could be taken by a seven and an eight. To break ties, players play two more cards. Their values alone break the tie; players don't add them to the two that are already faceup. Play continues until someone runs out of cards. The winner is then the player with the most cards. Or play goes for five minutes, and the winner is the player with the most cards at the end of that time.

Water Brigade

Type: Water-moving race
Object: Be the first team to fill its bucket first
Players: 4 or many more
Ages: 3 and older
Where: Outdoors!
Equipment: Wading pools or tubs, buckets, paper cups

Water Brigade is definitely a wet, outdoor, summertime race! The players divide into two teams and fill one or more large tubs or wading pools with water. Ten or more feet away, they line up buckets or small tubs (one for each team); they should hold the same amount of water and be level. Each player gets a paper or plastic cup and stands near the pool. Go! All at one time, the players run back and forth, carrying water from pool to their team's bucket.
The first team to fill its bucket wins.

Variation: Players need a (waterproof!) watch to run this relay race. They draw a start line, give each team a plastic or paper cup, and set up two buckets or tubs for each team. Both teams line up behind the start line. Go! The first runner fills the cup from the start bucket, runs and empties it into the target bucket, races back to his team, and passes the cup. The winning team is the one with the most water in its target bucket after three minutes.

228

Water Hoops

Type:	Pickup water-balloon basketball
Object:	Make goals, get points, wet your opponents
Players:	2 or more
Ages:	6 and older
Where:	Strictly outdoors in warm weather
Equipment:	A supply of water balloons; a basketball court or some homemade "baskets" (pails or plastic tubs)

Players can goof up their usual pickup basketball game by switching the basketballs for water balloons. For the player under the basket, the game of Twenty-One with water balloons gives dribbling an entire new meaning! Players can adapt any of their favorite games (Horse, Greedy, 'Round the World, Follow-Up Goal). However, since there's no real dribbling, players may take three—and only three—steps while holding the balloon. Then they must pass to a teammate or shoot.

Water Hoops can also be played on a lawn instead of on a basketball court. Four or more players place the "baskets" at opposite ends of the area and select a water balloon. If a player throws a balloon so hard it explodes in her teammate's hands, that's an out-of-bounds, and the next balloon goes to the other team. To block a shot, players may definitely step in front of the flying balloon and take the splash!

Water Volleyball

Type:	Volleyball in the water
Object:	Prevent the ball from hitting the water on your team's side
Players:	4 or more
Ages:	8 and older; comfortable in water
Where:	In a pool
Equipment:	Net or rope; volleyball or similar ball

The complete rules of regulation volleyball are detailed. For players who know them, moving the game to water is a cinch. But players new to volleyball can get started at Water Volleyball with just the basics. First, players divide into teams, mark off a court area in the water, then run a net or rope down the center. The court should be sized according to the number of players—and of course will be limited by the size of the available pool.

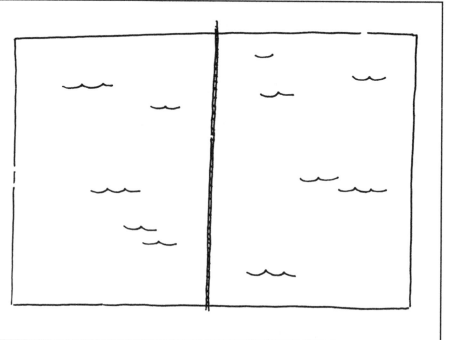

The basics of the game are simple. The teams get on each side of the net. Teams take turns serving the ball (batting it over the net with their hands for the first time). A serving player, positioned behind the last row of players on her team, may try three times to get the ball over the net. If she still can't make it, the ball goes to the other team. Once the ball is in play, both teams try to keep it up in the air, going back and forth over the net. This is the *volley*.

Team members may hit the ball
three times while it's on their side
of the net. After the third hit, it
must go over. During the three hits,
no one player may hit the ball twice
in a row.

If the ball escapes into the water
out of a player's hands, or a team
knocks it out of bounds, the other
team scores. Players should take
turns serving. Play continues until
one team wins by scoring 21.

Watermelon Ball

Type: Pool goal sport
Object: Get the melon to the opponent's corner
Players: 4–10 or so
Ages: 6 (tall enough and water-confident enough) and older
Where: In a pool
Equipment: A watermelon; petroleum jelly (optional)

The players designate a playing area in the pool. They divide into teams, choose sides of the area, and select goal corners. The players smear a watermelon with petroleum jelly (unless the pool owner objects) and set the melon floating in the center of the pool. The teams go to opposite sides.

Go! Everyone rushes to the watermelon and begins pushing. The object is to score by *pushing* the watermelon into the opponent's goal corner. Pushing only is allowed; players may not lift the melon out of the water and carry it. The team that gets the melon to the corner twice wins.

What's Missing?

Type: Memory
Object: Remember a set of objects well enough to spot the missing one
Players: 2 or more
Ages: 6 and older
Where: Anywhere
Equipment: Miscellaneous stuff (stamp, marble, pushpin, paper clip, dice, candy, coin, eraser, rubber band, bottle cap, twist tie, etc.); watch with a second hand or stopwatch

Get the miscellaneous stuff together in a bowl or basket. Dozens of different things are great. One player (It) chooses a certain number of objects—for example, six for six-year-olds. He lays them out and gives the other players twenty or thirty seconds to memorize the things. Then the players turn their backs and count to ten while It removes *one* of the things. The others turn around and look; the first one to name the missing object wins. Only one guess is allowed per player. If a player names the wrong thing, she's out. With just two players, they can play against the clock. They take turns being It with the same number of objects. The winner is the player who names the missing object the quickest on her turn.

Test for the reader: Examine the first picture for a few seconds. Now cover it and look at the second picture.

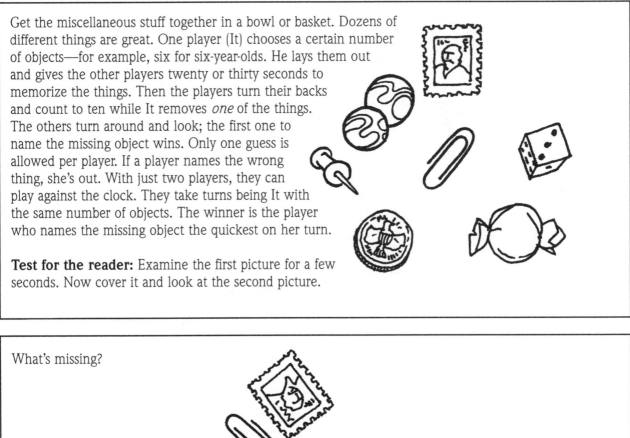

What's missing?

233

What's the Time, Mr. Wolf?

Type: Chase and tag
Object: Avoid getting caught by Mr. Wolf
Players: 4 or more
Ages: 3 and older
Where: Outdoors, gym
Equipment: None

One player is Mr. Wolf. The other players stand at a "safe" spot they have selected. Mr. Wolf strolls off away from the other players. They tease him, calling out, "What's the time, Mr. Wolf? What's the time?"

Then they begin to follow—but not too closely—behind him. They tease him, calling out, "What's the time, Mr. Wolf?" Mr. Wolf strolls on, answering, "Noon" or "Three o'clock" or "Five o'clock." Mr. Wolf tries to lure them farther and farther from the safe spot.

Suddenly Mr. Wolf turns and shouts, "Dinnertime!" The others race back to the safe spot. The first player caught becomes the new Mr. Wolf.

Variation: Players may, as they are caught, be forced to sit out in an area designated as the Wolf's den until everyone is caught in several rounds of play. The last player caught chooses the next Mr. Wolf.

Wheeled Toss-in Race

Type: Race on wheels
Object: Hit the most targets in the least time
Players: 2 or more
Ages: Able to wheel it
Where: A traffic-free, paved or packed-dirt open area
Equipment: Wheels (skates, skateboard, bicycle, or tricycle); balls and bags for the toss-in; watch with second hand or stopwatch

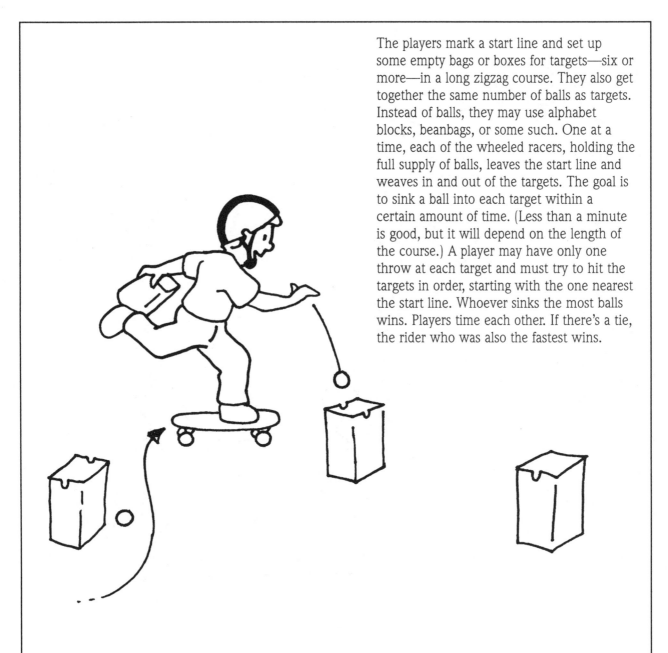

The players mark a start line and set up some empty bags or boxes for targets—six or more—in a long zigzag course. They also get together the same number of balls as targets. Instead of balls, they may use alphabet blocks, beanbags, or some such. One at a time, each of the wheeled racers, holding the full supply of balls, leaves the start line and weaves in and out of the targets. The goal is to sink a ball into each target within a certain amount of time. (Less than a minute is good, but it will depend on the length of the course.) A player may have only one throw at each target and must try to hit the targets in order, starting with the one nearest the start line. Whoever sinks the most balls wins. Players time each other. If there's a tie, the rider who was also the fastest wins.

Word Association

Type: Word
Object: See where you go
Players: 2 or more
Ages: 5 and older
Where: On a car trip or anywhere
Equipment: None

Simple Word Association goes like this: One player picks a word out of the blue and says it. Another responds with the first thing that pops into her mind. Players shouldn't let themselves "think" —just quickly say the first thing that comes to mind:

tree: bird
fly: sky
jet: ski
slope: hill
beans: rice
gravy: sauce
pan: pot
hole: half
cut: knife
gun: bullet . . .
and on and on.

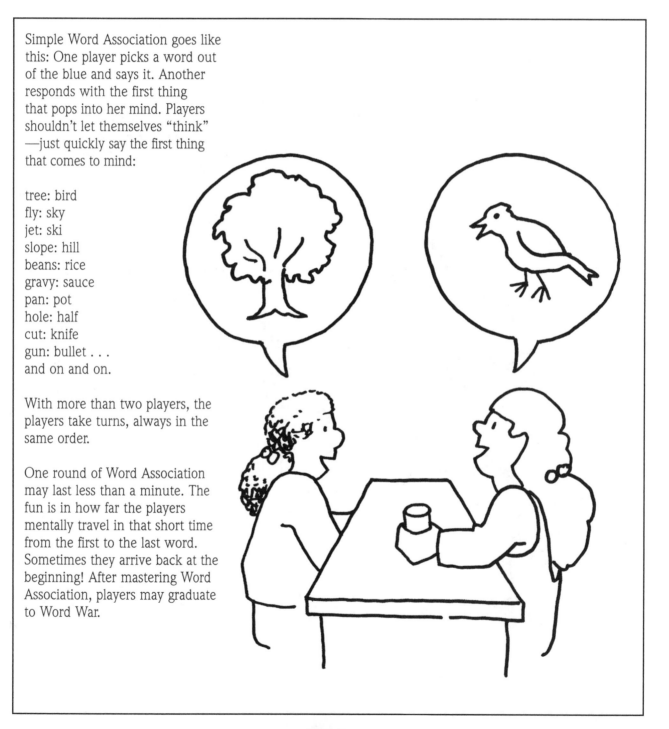

With more than two players, the players take turns, always in the same order.

One round of Word Association may last less than a minute. The fun is in how far the players mentally travel in that short time from the first to the last word. Sometimes they arrive back at the beginning! After mastering Word Association, players may graduate to Word War.

Word War

Type: Word
Object: Give great word clues for low score
Players: 3
Ages: 7 and older
Where: On a car trip or anywhere
Equipment: Pencil and paper

For this competitive version of Word Association, one player is the cluegiver, one the scorekeeper, and one the guesser for each round. At the beginning of each round, the cluegiver and the scorekeeper each choose a word, write it down, then show each other their words (let's say *blue* and *sailboat*). The guesser does not see the words.

To start, the cluegiver tells the guesser *one* of the words: blue. The guesser responds with the first thing that comes to mind: ocean. The cluegiver continues giving the guesser one-word clues, trying to lead the guesser to say "sailboat." The cluegiver may only give *one-word* clues at a time; the guesser may only respond one word at a time. The scorekeeper, meanwhile, records a mark for every clue given, not including the initial clue (blue). The cluegiver's score is the number of clues given by the cluegiver before the guesser says "sailboat." (Players may set a limit on how many clues the cluegiver is allowed. If the guesser hasn't gotten there in ten—or fifteen—tries that's the cluegiver's score. On to the next round.)

At each round, two new words are chosen, and the players change jobs from guesser to scorekeeper to cluegiver. When every player has had every job twice (each having the chance to score twice), they total their scores. Low score wins.

Zookeeper

Type:	Drawing
Object:	Make something from "nothing"
Players:	2 or more
Ages:	8 and older
Where:	On a car trip or anywhere
Equipment:	Pencils and paper

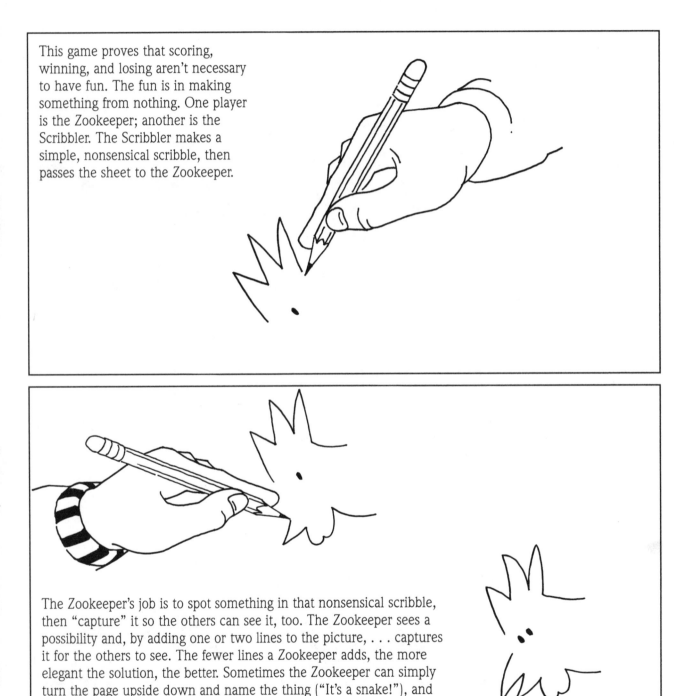

This game proves that scoring, winning, and losing aren't necessary to have fun. The fun is in making something from nothing. One player is the Zookeeper; another is the Scribbler. The Scribbler makes a simple, nonsensical scribble, then passes the sheet to the Zookeeper.

The Zookeeper's job is to spot something in that nonsensical scribble, then "capture" it so the others can see it, too. The Zookeeper sees a possibility and, by adding one or two lines to the picture, . . . captures it for the others to see. The fewer lines a Zookeeper adds, the more elegant the solution, the better. Sometimes the Zookeeper can simply turn the page upside down and name the thing ("It's a snake!"), and the others see it too. Players take turns being Zookeeper and Scribbler.

Subject Index

Active Nonball Games for Outdoors and Gyms
Apple Bobbing
Backlash
Beanbag Toss
Egg or Water-Balloon Toss
Frisbee Golf
Hat Thieves
Hide-and-Seek
Hide-and-Seek and Go Home
Hot Potato
Kick the Can
King of the Hill
Lean-Two
Leapfrog
Prisoner Base
Red Light, Green Light
Red Rover
Sardines
Seven Up
Statues
Tug-of-War
Ultimate Frisbee
Volcano

Ball Games for Big Groups
Ball Volley
Brooklyn Bridge
Caterpillar
Dodge War
Dodgeball
Dodgeball Reverse
German
German Singles
Goal Kickers
Greek Ball
Hand Tennis
Keep-Away
Pass Ball
Punch Ball
Squareball
Throw and Go
Toss Ball

Ball Games for Fewer Players
Ball and Caps
Four Square
Handball
Indian Ball

Minicroquet
Monkey in the Middle
Rosemary
Sidewalk Golf
Soccer Tag
Spud
Tree Ball
Trips
Trips, Jr.

Bicycle and Other Wheeled Games
Bicycle Beanbag Balance
Bicycle Coast Race
Bicycle Slalom Race
Bicycle Un-Race
Skate Obstacle Course
Wheeled Toss-in Race

Car Trip Games
Alphabet Objects
Battle at Sea
Botticelli
Catch a Cootie
Categories
Chain Story
Cootie-Bug
Drop Dead
Exquisite Corpse
Hangman
Homonyms
Homonym Detective
Homonyms in the Teakettle

Card Games
Crazy Eights
Deadly Queen
I Doubt It
Spoons
War
War Times Two

Hopscotch
Classic Hopscotch
English Hopscotch
Tic Tac Hopscotch

Hunt and Searching Games
Hide-and-Seek

Hide-and-Seek and Go Home
Hide the Button
Huckleberry Finn
Sardines
Scavenger Hunt
What's Missing?

Jacks
Eggs in the Basket
Onesies Twosies
Pigs in the Pen
Scrubs
Sheep over the Fence

Marbles
Bossout
Chasies
Hundreds
Obstacle Course
Poison Ring
Potsies
Ring and Line
Ringer
Spangie
Straight Shot
Tic Tac Taw

Milk Caps
Basic Caps
Bomb
Freeze!
Magic
Poison
Terminator
Threesies
Twosies

Mind, Word, and Memory Games
Adverbally
Alphabet Objects
Anagrams
Botticelli
Categories
Chain Story
Charades
Hangman
Homonyms
Homonym Detective
Homonyms in the Teakettle

I Spy
Memory
Mnemonics
Shopping Trip
Spell It How? (Llep Stiw Oh?)
Teacher's Cat
Telephone Message
Tell a Tale
Three Words
Twenty Questions
Virginia Woolf
What's Missing?
Word Association
Word War

Paper Games
Battle at Sea
Bingo
Bingo for Preschoolers
Catch a Cootie
Cootie-Bug
Exquisite Corpse
Pig in the Pen
Tic-Tac-Toe
Tic-Tac-Toe Four
Zookeeper

Pickup Basketball Games
Follow-Up Goal
Greedy
Horse
'Round the World
Twenty-One
Water Hoops

Pool Games
Chicken Fights
Killer Whale
Marco Polo
Moby Dick
Poison Ball
Shark and Minnows
Underwater Tag
Water Volleyball
Watermelon Ball

Races and Relay Races
Bad Sport's Race
Ball Duck Race
Balloon Duo
Bubble Blow Race

Cracker Race
Jambalaya Relay
Obstacle Course
Peanut Race
Potato Relay
Relay Race (Classic Version)
Water Brigade

Rainy Day Sports
Arm Wrestling
Cardywinks
Egg Polo
Hand Wrestling
Hundred-Mile Race
Paper Airplane Race
Simon Says
Simon Says *Not*
Thumb Wrestling
Volleyballoon

Suitable for Players Younger than Six
Ball Tag
Balloon Duo
Bingo for Preschoolers
Brooklyn Bridge
Cat and Mouse
Cross Tag
Drop the Hankie
Duck, Duck, Goose
Farmer, Farmer, May We Cross?
Fox and Hen
Freeze Tag
Fruit Basket
Grab Tag
Hide-and-Seek
Hide-and-Seek and Go Home
Hide the Button
Homonyms
Huckleberry Finn
Hundred-Mile Race
Jingle Tag
Kick the Can
Killer Whale
Lean-Two
Leapfrog
London Bridge
Moby Dick
Mother, May I?
Mousetrap
Mulberry Bush

Musical Chairs
Paper Airplane Race
Peanut Race
Poison
Poison Ball
Potato Relay
Red Light, Green Light
Relay Race (Classic Version)
Ring-Around-the-Rosy
Run for Your Supper
Safe Tag
Scissors, Paper, Stone
Shadow Tag
Sheep, Sheep, Come Home
What's the Time, Mr. Wolf?

Tag and Chase
Ball Tag
Blindman's Buff
Cross Tag
Freeze Tag
Fruit Basket
Grab Tag
Jingle Tag
Musical Chairs
Octopus
Pie Tag
Poison
Rabbit
Rattlesnake
Run for Your Supper
Safe Tag
Safety Zones
Tag
Wall of China

Trickery and Chance
Assassin
Black Magic
Catch a Cootie
Drop Dead